Joseph Viktor von Scheffel

The Trumpeter of Säkkingen

A song from the upper Rhine

Joseph Viktor von Scheffel

The Trumpeter of Säkkingen
A song from the upper Rhine

ISBN/EAN: 9783337318970

Printed in Europe, USA, Canada, Australia, Japan

Cover: Foto ©Thomas Meinert / pixelio.de

More available books at **www.hansebooks.com**

THE
TRUMPETER OF SÄKKINGEN

A Song from the Upper Rhine.

BY

JOSEPH VICTOR VON SCHEFFEL.

TRANSLATED FROM THE GERMAN BY

MRS. FRANCIS BRÜNNOW.

Translation authorised by the Poet.

London:
CHAPMAN AND HALL, 193, PICCADILLY.
NEW YORK: SCRIBNER, ARMSTRONG, & CO.
1877.

CHARLES DICKENS AND EVANS,
CRYSTAL PALACE PRESS.

O Song, at home well known to fame,
    That German hearts hath deeply stirred,
And long hath made of Scheffel's name
    A dear and honoured household word,

Go forth in thy first foreign dress,
    Go forth to Albion's noble land !
Will she not greetings kind express,
    And warmly clasp the stranger's hand ?

The Emerald Isle will surely give
    A welcome neither cold nor faint;
For on thy pages still doth live
    The name of Erin's ancient Saint.

Across the sea my country's shores
    As Hope's bright star before me rise ;
Will she not open wide her doors
    To one who on her heart relies ?

Farewell, oh work of vanished hours ;
    When suffering rent my weary heart,
Thy breath of fragrant woodland flowers
    Did life renew, fresh strength impart.

Oh Scheffel ! may thy years be long !
    And may'st thou live to see the time,
When this thy genial Schwarzwald song
    Will find a home in every clime.

Basel, June, 1877.

CONTENTS.

	PAGE
DEDICATION	1
PREFACE TO THE SECOND EDITION . .	7
PREFACE TO THE THIRD EDITION . . .	11
PREFACE TO THE FOURTH EDITION . .	13
PREFACE TO THE FIFTIETH EDITION . .	16

FIRST PART.
How young Werner rode into the Schwarzwald   19

SECOND PART.
Young Werner with the Schwarzwald Pastor .   33

THIRD PART.
St. Fridolin's Day   48

FOURTH PART.
Young Werner's Adventures on the Rhine   64

FIFTH PART.
The Baron and his Daughter   78

SIXTH PART.
How young Werner became the Baron's Trumpeter   94

SEVENTH PART.
The Excursion to the Mountain Lake. . .   109

CONTENTS.

EIGHTH PART.

	PAGE
The Concert in the Garden Pavilion	128

NINTH PART.

Teaching and Learning	142

TENTH PART.

Young Werner in the Gnome's Cave	153

ELEVENTH PART.

The Hauenstein Riot	169

TWELFTH PART.

Young Werner and Margaretta	187

THIRTEENTH PART.

Werner sues for Margaretta	201

FOURTEENTH PART.

The Book of Songs	215
Young Werner's Songs	217
Songs of the Cat Hiddigeigei	232
Songs of the Silent Man	247
Some of Margaretta's Songs	253
Werner's Songs. Five Years later	257

FIFTEENTH PART.

The Meeting in Rome	273

SIXTEENTH PART.

Solution and End	288
Notes	303

DEDICATION.

"Who is yonder light-haired stranger
Who there like a cat is roaming
O'er the roof of Don Pagano?"—
Thus asked many honest burghers,
Dwellers on the Isle of Capri,
When they from the market turning
Looked up at the palm-tree and the
Low-arched roof of moorish fashion.

And the worthy Don Pagano
Said: "That is a strange queer fellow,
And most strange his occupation.
Came here with but little luggage,
Lives here quite alone but happy,
Clambers up the steepest mountains,
Over cliffs, through surf is strolling,
Loves to steal along the sea-shore.
Also lately 'mid the ruins

Of the villa of Tiberius
With the hermits there caroused.
What's his business?—He's a German,
And who knows what they are doing?
But I saw upon his table
Heaps of paper written over,
Leaving very wasteful margins;
I believe he is half crazy,
I believe he's making verses."

Thus he spoke.—And I myself was
This queer stranger. Solitary
I had on this rocky island
Sung this song of my dear Schwarzwald.
I went as a wand'ring scholar
To far countries, to Italia;
With much art became acquainted,
Also with bad vetturinos,
And with many burning flea-bites;
But the sweet fruit of the lotus,
Which doth banish love of country
And the longing to return there,
I have never found here growing.

'Twas in Rome. Hard lay the winter
On th' eternal sev'n-hilled city:
Hard—for even Marcus Brutus
Would have caught a bad catarrh then;
And the rain seemed never-ending.

DEDICATION.

Like a dream then rose the vision
Of the Schwarzwald, and the story
Of the young musician Werner
And the lovely Margaretta.
In my youth I have stood often
By their graves close to the Rhine shore;
Many things which lie there buried
Are, however, long forgotten.
But like one to whom a sudden
Ringing in his ears betokens
That at home of him they're thinking,
So I heard young Werner's trumpet
Through the Roman Winter, through the
Carnival's gay flower-show—
Heard it from afar, then nearer,
Like the crystal which of vap'rous
Fine materials is condensing
And increases radiating ;
So the figures of this song grew—
Even followed me to Naples.
In the halls of the Museum
Who should meet me but the Baron
Shaking his big cane and smiling,
And before Pompeii's gate sat
The black tom-cat Hiddigeigei.
Purring, quoth he : " Leave all study ;
What is all this ancient rubbish,
E'en that dog there in mosaic
In the tragic Poet's dwelling,

In comparison with me—the
Epic type of all cat-nature?"

This I could no longer stand, so
Now began this ghost to banish.
From the brother of the lovely
Luisella, from the crooked
Cunning druggist of Sorrento
Quantities of ink I ordered,
And sailed o'er the bay to Capri.
Here began my exorcisms.
Many pale-gold coloured sea-fish,
Many lobsters, many oysters,
I ate up without compassion;
Drank the red wine like Tiberius,
Without mercy poetising;
On the roof went up and down till
All resounded metrically,
And the charm was then accomplished:
Chained up in four-measured trochees
Lay those figures which so long now
From my couch sweet sleep had banished.

'Twas high time, too; Spring already
Now gave signal of his coming—
Buds were sprouting on the fig-trees;
Shots were cracking, for with guns and
Nets they were the quails pursuing,
Who towards home their flight were taking;

DEDICATION.

And the minstrel was in peril
Then of seeing feathered colleagues
Set upon the table roasted.
This dread o'er him, pen and inkstand
Flew against the wall together.
Ready now and newly soled were
My strong boots which old Vesuvius
Had much damaged with his sulphur.
Farther now I journey onward.
Up, my good old Marinaro!
Off from land! the waves with pleasure
Bear light hearts and weightless freightage.

But the song, which with such happy
Spring-born feelings from my heart welled,
Bears my greetings to my country
And to you, my honoured parents.
Many faults are in it, truly:
Tragic pathos may be wanting,
And a racy tendance; also,
As in Amaranth, the fragrant
Incense of a pious soul, its
Sober but pretentious colouring.
Take him, as he is, this ruddy,
Rough, uncouth son of the mountains,
With a pine branch on his straw hat.
What he's wanting in, pray, cover
With the veil of kind indulgence.
Take him not as thanks, for always

In your Book of Love I'm debtor,
But as greeting and as witness,
That a man whom worldly fortune
Has not placed 'mid smiling verdure,
Yet can, happy as a lark pour
Out his song on leafless branches.

Capri, *May 1st*, 1853.

PREFACE

TO THE SECOND EDITION.

FIVE years, my merry song, have now rolled by
   Since thou didst venture thy first course to run,
A simple strolling minstrel's chance to try,
   But no great laurels so far hast thou won.
In circles of prosaic breathing mortals
   No praise was given thee of any kind—
Where formal stiffness bars life's glowing portals,
   Thou and thy kindred can no quarter find.
And in the coteries of hoops and laces
Few were the readers, fewer still the praises.

Not everything suits everyone: the hill
   Grows different flowers than the vale and lea:
But here and there in German homes there will
   Be found some hearts who fondly turn to thee;

Where merry fellows are their wine enjoying
    With cheerful songs, thy praises will resound ;
Near landscape-painters' easels thou art lying,
    And in a huntsman's bag thou oft art found,
And e'en of pastors it has been reported
To thee as to their prayer-books they've resorted.

And many who have taken a young bride
    To spend the honeymoon 'midst rural scenes,
Do like to read thee, sitting side by side ;
    Of happy hours thou often art the means.
Then Säkkingen, the fair Black Forest's treasure,
    Which found at first in thee not much delight,
Has by degrees derived from thee great pleasure,
    And to her heart with love has pressed thee tight.
Upon the whole, success outweighs detraction,
And thou canst view thy fate with satisfaction.

Now that thou wilt a second course begin,
    I should for thee a better dress prepare,
With finer threads the verses' measure spin,
    Here lengthen out, there shorten with more care.
I know it well, right often have I faltered,
    Some of thy trochees sound a little lame ;
But the old humour now, alas ! is altered,
    The mood which gave thee birth is not the same.
O rosy dreams of youth, when joy abounded,
Wherefore so soon by gloomy clouds surrounded !

PREFACE.

Once more in my dear Schwarzwald I now rest,
    And near me rush the healing waters out,
On high a bird of prey soars o'er his nest,
    And in the brook are sporting tiny trout.
From charcoal kilns the smoke clouds are ascending,
    With iris-coloured hues the sun embrace,
And stately giant pines in rows unending,
    Like wreaths of evergreens, the mountains grace.
A spicy hay-scent rises from the meadow,
And honest folk dwell 'neath their thatched roof's shadow.

And yet—should I now try new songs to sing,
    The old accustomed tone I could not find;
Too often grief my soul with pangs doth wring,
    Instead of mirth, scorn filleth now my mind.
The world serves idols now, the good ignoring,
    And truth is silent, beauty hides her face;
What is unnatural men are adoring,
    God is forgotten, Mammon takes his place!
The Poet, now, should be a prophet warning,
Like those of old, reproving, praying, mourning!

'Tis not *my* sphere; a mighty stirring song
    Requires another man, a different art;
But though so much prevails that's sad and wrong,
    One may not quite disdain a merry heart.

Go forth, my song, then, as thou didst before,
    A cheerful memory of life's fresh spring;
Cheer up those hearts, which grief made sad and sore,
    And to friends far and near my greeting bring.
Whenever men to nobler aims aspire,
Then higher too will ring the poet's lyre.

Rippoldsau, *September*, 1858.

PREFACE

TO THE THIRD EDITION.

HIDDIGEIGEI, his opinion :
  "Strange, perverse, are all mankind,
Who, when discord holds dominion,
  In such ditties pleasure find. . . .
Questions which the world are shaking,
  Now the thinker's mind assail,
And no light as yet is breaking,
  Which solution shall prevail.

"Yet our song unto perdition
  Has not been condemned, I hear—
What a marvel !—an edition
  For the third time will appear.
Which in new dress, not inferior
  (Of the old nought has been spared),
And, with quite unchanged interior,
  For its third trip is prepared.

"I regret that I'm declining,
  And I fear I have the mange;
And I show now, by my whining,
  When the wind and weather change.
Coming storms, when brewing, ever
  My keen senses do betray;
And the atmosphere was never
  Sultry as it is to-day.

"Doubly thus I feel this parting,
  But thy course must onward lead;
Take my blessing, song, on starting,
  And the cat's well-meant good speed!
The green Rhine, the Schwarzwald breezes,
  Bring with them health, peace, and rest;
Such a merry fellow pleases,
  And is hailed a welcome guest.

"Golden Spring, thee still I'm praising;
  When the trumpet-notes rang out,
Then my bristling fur seemed blazing,
  And bright sparks flew all about;
And the trumpet with my growling
  Then defied Fate's evil doom;
Gentle is to-day my howling
  O'er the hidden future's gloom."

Summer, 1862.

PREFACE

TO THE FOURTH EDITION.

THE Boezberg for the Rhine I have been leaving,
  A home-sick longing stirred my heart within,
Once more that fragrant air I would be breathing
  Again would see the town of Fridolin.
As if at my return with joy elated,
  She lay there basking in the autumn sun,
Her minster's towers lately renovated,
  Reflected in the river, brightly shone;
Far to the North, through bluish vapour breaking.
The Hozzenwald, a stately background making.

From the Gallus-Thurm on the Roman wall erected,
  To where the ancient convent buildings lie,
The well-known gable roofs I all detected,
  Where often my light skiff had glided by;
And where the shore by gravel banks is bounded.
  A sunny garden's blooming face doth smile;
Half hidden by the chestnuts which surround it
  Lies cosily the castle's graceful pile.

To it my hat in greeting I am tossing,
As o'er the ancient covered bridge I'm crossing.

Unto the dead my steps at first were tending,
    Unto the graveyard where the Rhine flows by,
For many had been called to rest unending,
    Who once with me enjoyed this balmy sky.
The old stone wall I neared with deep emotion,
    Inscribed with Werner Kirchhof's name and arms,
And of his wife a record of devotion,
    Which, though long past, e'en now attracts and charms.
And Heaven's blessing on the pair alighted,
By death the same year they were re-united.

To the market then I turned. "Are ghosts here wandering,
    Or is it you yourself who meets mine eyes?"
So said the mayor by the court-house standing,
    Who slowly did the stranger recognise. . . .
Long years have passed since friends were often going
    To hear my judgments in the dusky court;
But though now many heads gray locks are showing,
    Their hearts are fresh, their memory is not short;
And as we never shunned good cheer and drinking,
From foaming bumpers we'll not now be shrinking.

'Tis true the Button landlord has been moving
    Out of his cosy tavern on the Square,
But still retains his former skill in brewing,
    And in his new inn keeps the same good fare.

And as around the table we sat cheering
  Our hearts with kindly memories of old,
From many lips I these glad news was hearing,
  Which please the Poet more than heaps of gold :
The Trumpeter, whose story I'd been singing,
To young and old more joy was daily bringing.

As a vignette the weekly paper gracing
  He's blowing politics instead of music now ;
And even more, somebody has been placing
  My hero on the stage—but ask not how.
Could I but see the walls of the new tower,
  Which now is rising in the old one's place,
Embellished by an artist of great power—
  The figures of my song devised with grace !
Thus might an artist's hand make expiation
For the abuse by stage-representation.

However, let that go, I am not fearing
  Whatever purpose thou mayst serve my song ;
Now that a new edition is appearing,
  I send my greeting home with it along.
On thy fourth tour thou Schwarzwald-child be hieing,
  Where truth and goodness dwell, there enter in,
And preach to those who with *ennui* are sighing,
  How innocent amusement they may win.
As often as there comes a new edition,
"Preserve thee, God !" be ever my petition.

Seon in the Aargau, *November*, 1864.

PREFACE

TO THE FIFTIETH EDITION.

The Trumpeter now, all alive and refreshed,
   To the Jubilee loudly is blowing;
The present year has both of us blessed,
   Great favour and lustre bestowing.
I have my fiftieth year attained,
   Through joy and through sorrow surviving,
And his editions—such fame has he gained—
   At the fiftieth are now arriving.

It may be that I a part of my youth
   And joy with him have been leaving;
But still from these scenes—to tell the truth—
   Great pleasure I now am receiving.
To the Eggberg I climbed, where on high are seen
   The homes of the Hauenstein peasant;
Their straw-thatched roofs with mosses still green,
   But no more quaint costumes at present.

Through gaps in the forest I see shining bright
   The snow-peaks of Switzerland's Giants,
The steep Finsteraarhorn's towering height
   The Jungfrau dazzling with diamonds;
And as to the west I turn my gaze,
   Blue ridge above ridge is unfolding;
And, in the evening's golden haze,
   I'm the Vosges' great Belchen beholding.

When now to Säkkingen downward I hie,
   Through the dark green forest is gleaming
The silvery lake, like the earth's clear eye,
   Looking upward, invitingly beaming.
Gneiss rocks high o'er the grassy shore rise;
   And placed so as best to show it,
Inscribed on a rock this meets mine eyes:
   "Säkkingen, the town, to her Poet!"

And now, as by Bally's castle I stand,
   There my Trumpeter also stands blowing,
Cast finely in bronze by a master's hand.
   That they know us well here all are showing;
For, when I was going to pay at the inn,
   The kind hostess refused quite indignant.
'Tis clear, in the town of St. Fridolin,
   O'er us a bright star shines benignant.

The Trumpeter bravely has blown his way
    Through much that his patience was tasking;
And the publisher also his joy doth betray:
    For the author's likeness he's asking.
Accept then this book, my friends, as before,
    With kind and growing affection;
When the Schwarzwald's Poet shall be no more,
    Still hold him in fond recollection.

Carlsruhe, *October*, 1876.

THE TRUMPETER OF SÄKKINGEN.

FIRST PART.

HOW YOUNG WERNER RODE INTO THE SCHWARZWALD.

To the Schwarzwald soars my song, up
To the Feldberg, where the last small
Cluster of its comrade mountains
Toward the south are boldly looking,
And, all mailed in fir-tree armour,
Keep good watch there on the Rhine.

Be thou greeted, peaceful forest!
Be ye greeted, ancient pine-trees,
Ye, who oft beneath your shadow
Me, the weary one, have sheltered.
Oddly twisted, spread your roots down

Deep within the earth's vast bowels,
Strength from out those depths imbibing,
While to us is closed the entrance.
And you envy not a transient
Human being's transient doings,
Only smile ;—his feast at Christmas
You adorn with your young scions.
In your sturdy trunks lives also
Conscious life-sustaining power.
Resin through your veins is coursing ;
And your dreamy thoughts are surging
Slow and heavy, upward, downward.
Oft I saw the clear and gummy
Tears which from your bark were oozing,
When a woodman's wanton axe-stroke
Rudely felled some loved companion.
Oft I heard your topmost summits
Spirit-like together whisper.
Then there breathed throughout my soul a
Sweet mysterious solemn dreaming.
Don't find fault then, if my song now
Soars within the forest shades.

 'Twas in March : still played the Winter
Masquerade ; the branches, laden
With fantastical ice-crystals,
To the ground were lowly drooping ;
Here and there, out of Earth's bosom
Tender plants their heads were thrusting—-

Wood-anemones and cowslips.
As the patriarch, old Noah,
At the time of the great Deluge,
Sent the dove to reconnoitre:
So with winter's ice sore burdened,
With impatience sends the Earth forth
These first flowers with a question,
Asking, whether the oppressor
Has not come to his last gasp yet.
Blustering from the Feldberg's summit
Now old Master Storm is rushing,
And rejoices, through the dark dense
Forest he again is blowing;
Says: " I greet you, ancient comrades;
Why I come, you know the reason—
They believe, poor mortal children,
When they see me tearing, snatching
Roughly some old hat away,
I am only there to frighten.
That would be a pretty business,
Breaking chimneys, smashing windows,
Scattering through the air some thatchings,
Tearing some old woman's clothing
Till she signs the cross in praying!
But you fir-trees know me better,
Me, the fair Spring's thorough cleaner,
Who what's mouldy sweeps afar off—
Who what's rotten blows to pieces—
Who the earth's domain well cleanses,

That his radiant Lord and Master
Worthily may make his entrance.
And you, noble forest comrades,
Who so oft, with bronze-like foreheads,
Bravely have withstood my rudeness,
Ye whose trunks I have to thank for
Many knocks against my skull-bone,
Ye alone shall hear my secret:
Soon the Spring himself he cometh,
And then, when the buds are bursting,
Lark and blackbird sing their carols,
And with fervent heat the Spring sun
Brightly on your heads is shining,
Then remember me, the Storm-wind,
Who to-day, with boisterous fury
As his harbinger swept past."

Speaking thus, he shook the tree-tops
With great roughness; boughs are snapping,
Branches falling, and a thick, fine
Rain of pine-leaves crackles downward.
But the fir-trees, quite indignant,
Took small notice of this homage.
From their summits rang the answer,
Rather scolding, I should call it:
"You unmannerly rude fellow!
We will have no business with you,
And regret much that the finest
Lords have oft the rudest servants.

To the Alps begone directly,
There is sport fit for your humour;
There stand walls of rock all barren;
Entertain yourself with them there."

   Now, while thus the storm and fir-trees
Held such converse with each other,
Could be heard a horse's footfall.
Toiling through the snow-piled wood-path
Seeks his way a weary horseman;
Gaily flutters in the storm-wind,
To and fro, his long gray mantle,
His fair curling locks are waving,
And, from out the cocked-up hat there
Boldly nods a heron's feather.
On his lips was just appearing
Such a downy beard as ladies
Much admire, because it showeth
That its bearer is a man, still
One whose kisses will not wound them.
But not many pretty lips had
Felt the soft touch of this beard yet,
Which, as if for fun and mischief,
Snow and ice now decked with crystals.
In his clear blue eyes were glowing
Warmth and mildness, earnest meaning,
And you could not doubt his fist would
Strike a valiant blow, when needed,
With the heavy basket-hilted

Sword, which, worn suspended by a
Black belt from his shoulder, well-nigh
Grazed the ground as he was riding.
Wound around his riding-doublet
Was a sash, to which was tied the
Richly-gilded shining trumpet,
Which he often with his mantle
Sheltered from the falling snow-flakes;
But, whene'er the wind pierced through it,
Bringing forth tones shrill and wailing;
Then around his mouth there played a
Sweet strange smile of melancholy.

 Silent through the forest's thicket
On he rode, while often roving
Were his glances—as the case is,
When a wanderer for the first time
Over unknown roads is travelling.
Rough the path—the poor horse often
In the snow was nearly sinking,
And o'er gnarl'd and tangled branches
Of the knotted pine-roots stumbling.
And the rider, in ill-humour,
Said: "Sometimes it is quite tedious,
Through the world alone to travel.
There are times, 'mid gloomy forests,
When one longeth for companions.
Since I bade farewell this morning
To the good monks of St. Blasien,

FIRST PART.

Lonely was the road and dreary.
Scattered here and there, a peasant,
Through the snow-storm running swiftly,
Hardly did my greeting notice.
Then a pair of coal-black ravens,
Who with hoarse discordant croakings,
O'er a dead mole fiercely quarrelled;
For the past two hours, however,
I not once have had the honour
To behold one living being.
And in this lone forest district,
Where the lofty snow-clad pine-trees
Look as if in shrouds enveloped,
I should like to have some comrades,
Were they even rogues or gipsies,
Or those two suspicious fellows
Who escorted the old knight once
Through the forest's gloom and thicket;
Then appeared as Death and Devil,
Grinning in his face with scorn!
I should rather ride with them now—
Rather fight them, or play lively
Dances for them, than so lonely
Thus to trot through this dense forest."

All comes to an end, however,
Even riding through the forests.
Round the trunks it grew much lighter,
Storm and snow-clouds were receding,

And the blue sky smiled benignant
Through the dense shade of the pine-woods.
Thus the miner, looking upward,
Sees, far at the pit's mouth shining,
Like a star, the distant daylight,
Which he greets with joyful shouting.
Likewise such a cheerful feeling
Brightens up our rider's face.
So he reached the forest's border,
And his eyes, so long restricted
By dark woods to narrow prospects,
Gladly swept the wide horizon.

O how lovely woods and fields lay!
Green meads in the narrow valley,
Straw-thatched huts, low-roofed and mossy,
And the modest village steeple;
Deep below, where dusky forests
Stretch along unto the lowlands,
Like a long bright streak of silver,
Takes the Rhine his westward course.
Far off from the island glisten
Battlements and lofty houses,
And the minster's two tall spires;
While beyond, in misty distance
Shining, rise up unto Heaven
Snowy peaks of giant mountains,
Guardians of Helvetia's soil,
As the pallid ardent thinker's

FIRST PART.

Eye doth glow and cheek doth redden,
When a thought, new and creative,
Through his brain has flashed like lightning,
So the golden light of evening
Glows upon the Alpine Giants.
(Do they dream of throes of labour
Which their mother-earth of old felt,
When they from her womb were bursting?)

   From the horse got off our rider,
To a pine-tree stump he bound it,
Gazed in wonder at the landscape,
Spoke no word, but shouting tossed up
In the air his pointed cocked hat.
And began to blow a cheering
Joyous tune upon his trumpet.
To the Rhine it bore a greeting,
Over toward the Alps it floated,
Merry now, then full of feeling,
Like a prayer devout and solemn,
Then again quite roguish, joyful.
Now trari-trara resounded,
Echo's voice her plaudits sending
From the bosom of the forest.
Fair it was o'er hill and valley,
But fair also to behold him,
As he in the deep snow standing
Lightly on his horse was leaning;
Now and then a golden sunbeam

Glory shed on man and trumpet,
In the background gloomy fir-trees,
Farther down among the meadows
Rang his tunes out not unheeded!
There was walking then the worthy
Pastor of the neighbouring village,
Who the snow-drifts was examining,
Which, fast melting with the surging
Waters rising o'er the meadows,
Threatened to destroy the grass there.
Plunged in thought, he deeply pondered
How to ward off this great danger.
Round him bounded, loudly barking,
His two white and shaggy dogs.

 You who live in smoky cities,
And are separated wholly
From the simple life of nature,
Shrug your shoulders! for my muse will
Joyfully now sing the praises
Of a pastor in the country.
Simple is his life, and narrow:
Where the village ends, end also
All his labours and endeavours.
While men slaughtered one another,
In the bloody Thirty Years' War,
For God's honour, the calm grandeur
Of the Schwarzwald's solemn pine-woods
Breathed its peace into his soul.

Spider-webs spread o'er his book-shelves;
And, 'mid all the theologians'
Squabbles, he most likely never
Had read one polemic treatise.
With dogmatics altogether,
Science in her heavy armour,
He possessed but slight acquaintance.
But, whenever 'mongst his people
Could some discord be adjusted—
When the spiteful neighbours quarrelled;
When the demon of dissension
Marriage marred and children's duty;
When the daily load of sorrow
Heavily weighed down some poor man,
And the needy longing soul looked
Eagerly for consolation—
Then, as messenger from Heaven,
To his flock the old man hastened;
From the depths of his heart's treasure
Gave to each advice and comfort.
And if, in a distant village,
Someone lay upon a sick-bed,
With grim Death hard battle waging,
Then—at midnight—at each hour,
When a knock came at his hall-door—
E'en if snow the pathway covered—
Undismayed he went to comfort
And bestow the sacred blessing.
Solitary was his own life,

For his nearest friends were only
His two noble dogs (St. Bernards).
His reward: a little child oft
Bashfully approached him, kissing
His old hand with timid reverence;
Also oft a grateful smile played
O'er the features of the dying,
Which was meant for the old priest.

 Unperceived the old man came now
By the border of the forest,
To the Trumpeter whose last notes
Rang resounding in the distance,
Tapped him friendly on the shoulder:
" My young master, may God bless you,
"Twas a fine tune you were playing!
Since the horsemen of the emperor
Buried here their serjeant-major,
Whom a Swedish cannon-ball had
Wounded mortally at Rhinefeld,
And they blew as a farewell then
The Reveille for their dead comrade—
Though 'tis long since it has happened,
I have never heard such sounds here.
Only on the organ plays my
Organist, and that quite poorly;
Therefore I am struck with wonder
To encounter such an Orpheus.
Will you treat to such fine music

The wild beasts here of our forest,
Stag and doe, and fox and badger?
Or, perhaps, was it a signal,
Like the call of the lost huntsman?
I can see that you are strange here,
By your long sword and your doublet;
It is far still to the town there,
And the road impracticable.
Look, the Rhine-fog mounts already
High up towards these upland forests,
And it seems to me but prudent
That with me you take your lodging;
In the vale there stands my glebe-house,
Plain, 'tis true, yet horse and rider
Find sufficient shelter there."

Then the horseman quickly answered:
"Yes, I'm strange in a strange country,
And I have not much reflected
Where to-night shall be my lodging.
To be sure, in these free forests
A free heart can sleep if need be:
But your courteous invitation
I most gratefully accept."

Then unfastened he his horse and
Led it gently by the bridle,
And the Pastor and the rider
Like old friends walked to the village

In the twilight of the evening.
By the window of the glebe-house
The old cook stood, looking serious;
Mournfully her hands she lifted,
Took a pinch of snuff and cried out:
" Good St. Agnes! good St. Agnes!
Stand by me in this my trouble!
Thoughtlessly my kind old master
Brings again a guest to stay here;
What a thorough devastation
Will he make in my good larder!
Now farewell, you lovely brook-trout,
Which I had reserved for Sunday,
When the Dean of Wehr will dine here.
Now farewell, thou hough of bacon!
The old clucking hen, I fear much,
Also now must fall a victim,
And the stranger's hungry horse will
Revel in our store of oats."

SECOND PART.

YOUNG WERNER WITH THE SCHWARZWALD PASTOR.

SNUGLY in the well-warmed chamber,
Now before the supper table,
Sat the Trumpeter and Pastor.
On the dish, right hot and steaming
Had a roasted fowl paraded,
But it had completely vanished;
Only now a spicy fragrance
Floated gently through the chamber,
Like the songs by which the minstrel
Still lives on through after ages;
And the empty plates bore witness
That a great and healthy hunger
Lately here had been appeased.

Now the Pastor raised a brimming
Jug of wine, then filled the glasses
And began, his guest accosting:
"After supper 'tis the duty

Of the host, his guest to question:
Who he is, from whence he cometh?
Where his country and his parents?
In old Homer I have read oft
That the King of the Phæacians
Thus the noble hero questioned;
And I hope you can relate me
Just as many strange adventures
As Ulysses. Take your comfort,
Seat yourself in that warm corner,
Yonder by the stove, which is a
Hatching nest of solid thinking;
'Tis according to our custom
The narrator's seat of honour,
And I'll listen with attention.
Still the old man hears with pleasure
Of the storms of youth's wild passions."

Then the young man: "I am sorry
Not to be a proven hero,
Neither have I conquered Ilium,
Nor have blinded Polyphemus,
Neither have I ever thus far
Met with any Royal Princess,
Who when spreading out the linen
Felt for me a soft compassion.
But with pleasure I obey you."
On the bench he took his seat now
By the stove all covered over

With glazed tiles much ornamented.
From the stove streamed out warm comfort,
And the Pastor kindly told him
To stretch out his weary legs there.
He, however, would not do so;
Took a swallow of the red wine,
And began to tell his story:

" Know, my name is Werner Kirchhof;
I was born and grew to manhood,
In the Pfalz, at Heidelberg."

Old Heidelberg, thou beauty,
  With many honours crowned;
Along the Rhine and Neckar,
  No town like thee is found.

Thou town of merry fellows,
  Of wisdom full and wine,
Clear flows thy placid river,
  Blue eyes therein do shine.

When from the south is spreading
  Spring's smile o'er hill and lea,
He out of blossoms weaveth
  A bridal robe for thee.

Thee as a bride I fondly
   Enshrine within my heart;
Like early love's sweet echoes,
   Thy name doth joy impart.

Become life's cares too burning,
   And all abroad looks bare,
I'll spur my good horse homeward
   To the Neckar vale so fair.

"On the borders of the Neckar
I have dreamt sweet dreams of childhood,
Also have a school attended,
Greek and Latin there have studied;
And a thirsty old musician
Taught me how to blow the trumpet.
When I reached my eighteenth birthday,
Said my guardian: 'You, young Werner,
With a clever head are gifted,
And are somewhat of a genius,
And cut out of right material;
You must now become a lawyer.
That brings office and great honours,
Gathers also golden ducats.
And already I do see you
As the well-appointed bailiff
Of His Grace the Grand Elector;
And I then must pay you homage.
I will venture the prediction,

If you act quite circumspectly,
Then a seat may yet await you
In th' Imperial Court at Wetzlar.'
Thus I then became a lawyer ;
Bought myself a great big inkstand,
Also bought a huge portfolio,
And a heavy Corpus Juris,
And the lecture-room frequented,
Where, with yellow mummy visage,
Samuel Brunnquell, the professor,
Roman law to us expounded.
Roman law, when I recall it,
On my heart it lies like nightmare,
Like a millstone on my stomach,
And my head feels dull and stupid.
To much nonsense did I listen,
How they in the Roman Forum
Snarling, quarrelled with each other ;
How Sir Gaius stuck to his point,
And to his Sir Ulpianus ;
How then later comers dabbled,
Till the Emperor Justinianus,
He of all the greatest dabbler,
Sent them home about their business.
And I often asked the question :
' Must it really be our fate then
These dry bones to gnaw forever,
Which were flung to us as remnants
From their banquets by the Romans ?

Why should not, from soil Germanic,
Spring the flower of her own law,
Simple, full of forest fragrance—
No luxuriant southern climber?
Sad fate of the late-born races!
Must read till their brows are sweating,
And must try to disentangle
Knotty twisted skeins forever.
Can't we have a sword to cut them?'

"Often, nightly, by the lamp-light
I sat poring o'er the Codex,
Read the Glossary and Cujacius
Till my weary brain was racking;
But this zeal brought me no blessing.
Merrily would then my thoughts fly
From my studies to that time when
Old Cujacius' lovely daughter
Mounted in her father's rostrum,
With her voice sweet and melodious,
Read for him his written lectures
To the lucky youth of Paris.
Usucaption and inheritance,
And Novella hundred and eighteen,
Changed into a dark-haired maiden
Peeping from the Corpus Juris.
From my trembling hands the pen fell,
Overturned were sand and inkstand,
And I caught hold of the trumpet:

Usucaption and inheritance,
And Novella hundred and eighteen,
Wailing in adagio tempo,
Flew forth from the study window
Far into the starry night.

"Yes, this zeal brought me no blessing.
I one day went from my lodging,
'Neath my arm the Corpus Juris
('Twas the Elzevir edition,
Which at Rotterdam was published)
To the Heugass', to the pawn-house,
Where the Jew, Levi Ben Machol,
With his squinting eyes rapacious,
Took it in his arms paternal,
Paid me then two golden ducats—
Someone else may now redeem it!
I became a saucy fellow,
Wandered much o'er hill and valley
Clinking spurs and serenading.
If I ever caught one sneering,
Quickly grasped my hand the rapier:
'Fight a duel! draw your weapons!
Now advance!' That whistled nicely
Through the air; on many smooth cheeks
Wrote my sword so sharp and steady
A memento everlasting.
I, however, must confess here,
That I did not choose the finest

Company to wander round with.
What I liked, was to sit drinking
Up in the Elector's Castle,
By our age's greatest marvel
Which the German mind has wrought out,
By the tun of Heidelberg.
A most worthy hermit dwelt there,
Who was the Elector's court fool,
Was my dear old friend Perkéo;
Who had out of life's wild whirlpool
Peacefully withdrawn himself where
He could meditate while drinking,
And the cellar was his refuge.
Here he lived, his care dividing
'Twixt himself and the big wine-tun;
And he loved it—truer friendship
Never has the world yet witnessed;
'Twas as if it were his bride.
With a broom he swept it shining,
Chased away the ugly spiders,
And whenever came a feast-day,
Hung it o'er with wreaths of ivy;
Sang to it the morning greeting,
Also sang the song of evening,
And he carved in wood the image
Of himself as his best offering.
But when sipping his reward then
From the big tun's mouth with kisses,
Forth he launched in flights of fancy.

Often at his feet I listened
To his odd and comic speeches :
'There above, they call me foolish,
Let them gossip, my dear fellow,
Gossip never doth annoy me.
Oh, the world has grown quite stupid !
How they grope, and how they stumble,
Over paths, to find what Truth is ;
Still in fog they are enveloped.
To the first cause of all being
We must needs go back, and bring the
Last result of our researches
In a concrete form together.
Thus we comprehend the world well ;
For this purpose I am drinking
Truly cosmogonically.
Mundane space to me is nothing
But a roomy vaultèd cellar,
Where as first and central wine-tun,
Firmly stands the sun erected !
Next to him the rank and file of
Smaller casks, fixed stars and planets.
As the divers casks are holding
Wines of various sorts and flavours,
So comprise the heavenly bodies
Various spiritual natures.
Land-wine this—that Rüdesheimer ;
But the earth-cask holds a mixture ;
Fermentation has half clouded

And half volatilised the spirit.
The antagony of matter
And of spirit is, by thinking,
Blended into higher union.
Thus soars my creative genius
Far on high, while I am drinking.
And when through my brain are rushing
Revelations from the wine-fumes,
And when then my feeble body
Tottering sinks down by the wine-tun,
'Tis the triumph of the spirit,
'Tis the act of self-deliverance
From the narrow bounds of being.
Thus my solitude doth teach me
Nature's everlasting system.
With mankind it would be better,
Had the great Germanic race but
Understood their high vocation,
And throughout the world had carried
High the standard of the wine-cask,
Made of drinking a devotion—
As the Persians worship fire !'
O Perkéo ! better were it
Now with me, if to thy wisdom
I had never, never listened !
'Twas a sharp cold winter morning,
When down in the cosy cellar
We were taking a potation,
Talking philosophically;

But when I stepped out at midday,
The whole world and everybody
Looked most strangely queer and funny.
Rosy hues lit up all Nature,
Angel-voices I heard plainly.
On the balcony of the castle
Stood surrounded by her ladies,
Full of grace, of all the fairest,
The Electress Leonora.
Up to her start my bold glances,
Up to her my daring longing;
Clouded was my understanding.
Quickly I approached the terrace
And began to sing the wild air
Which the Palsgrave Frederic once sang,
As a love-sick serenader,
To his lovely English bride."

I kneel to thee as thy faithful true knight,
Fair Princess, of women the pearl!
   Command, and I fight the Emperor's host,
   Command, and I hold the most dangerous
      post, .
To atoms the world I will hurl.

I'll fetch thee from Heaven the sun and the
   moon,
Fair Princess, of women the crown!

I'll fetch countless stars from yon azure
   height,
Spit them like frogs on my spear sharp and
   bright,
And low at your feet lay them down.

Command, I will even become a fool,
Fair Princess, of women the prize!
   Indeed, I am one already I see,
   The light is far too dazzling for me,
Which streams from thy sunny blue eyes.

     *   *   *   *   *

   " Do you hear the trumpets blowing?
Do you hear the cannon roaring?
There, near Prague, at Weissenberg, now
For Bohemia's throne they're fighting.
Palsgrave, 'twas a short sad winter!
Palsgrave, thou wast sore defeated!
Spur thy horse and seek a refuge!

   " O thou fairest of all women,
From my dream what an awaking!
For there came to me the Beadle,
Summoned me before the Rector.
Grimly wrinkled he his forehead,
Wild with rage his locks were shaking;
Sternly he pronounced my sentence—
His Magnificence the Rector:

'For your unpermitted blowing,
For your unpermitted sing-song
In the Castle's sacred precincts,
You must quit the town and college
In three days; by special favour
Of our gracious sovereign princess,
Further punishment is spared.'

"Leave the town now—was I dreaming?
No, it was a fact well founded.
But before I left the city,
All my debts I fully settled,
In such cases quite unusual;
And I rode on the third morning
Out of Heidelberg; the fourth day
Out of the Elector's country
Unoffended; though my home had
Thrust me out—the bolts drawn on me—
Yet I will not cease to love her.
And the trumpet, cause of mischief,
I hung gaily on my shoulder.
And I augur it shall yet peal
Joyful tunes to help me onward.
I don't know now to what haven
Horse and tempest may yet bear me,
Still I look not backward more.
Cheerful heart and courage daring
Knows no sorrow, nor despairing,
Fortune has good luck in store.

Thus I came into the Schwarzwald.—
My kind host, pray tell me frankly
Whether my long tale has made you
Feel a heavy sleep approaching.
But if not, I'll be most grateful
If you'll give me some advice."

Smiling rang the good old Pastor
Glass to glass, and smiling said he :
"Your tale has a lucky ending.
I remember quite another,
Of a young and handsome carpenter,
And a Margravine's allurements.
But it ended on the gallows.
In this case, I am much puzzled
How to give you good advice.
In my code it is not written
How to counsel such a person,
Who with songs insults fair ladies,
Leaves his law books in the pawn-house,
With his trumpet loudly bloweth
To himself a rosy future.
But when human knowledge faileth,
Heaven graciously doth help us.
Way down in the forest-city,
There in Säkkingen is a worthy
Patron saint of all young people,
Is the holy Fridolinus;

SECOND PART.

And to-morrow is his feast-day.
Never has he yet forsaken
Him who prays for help in trouble ;
Therefore ask Saint Fridolinus."

THIRD PART.

ST. FRIDOLIN'S DAY.

Lo! a ship comes o'er the ocean,
Near Franconia's coast approaching,
Foreign sails and foreign pendant.
At the rudder sits a pale man,
Clad in black and monkish robes.
Hollow, like a mournful wailing,
Sounds the strange speech of the pilgrims,
Sound their prayers, and cries of sailors.
'Tis the ancient Celtic language
From the Emerald Isle of Erin;
And the vessel bears the pious
Missionary Fridolinus.
"Cease thy grieving, dearest mother;
Not with sword nor with the war-axe
Shall thy son gain fame and honour:
Other ages, other weapons—
Faith and Love are my sole armour.
For the love I bear my Saviour

I go forth unto the heathen;
Celtic blood impels me onward.
And in dreams I've seen a vision—
A strange land and pine-clad mountains,
A clear stream with a green island,
Most as fair as my own country;
Thither points the Lord His finger,
Thither sails now Fridolinus."

With a few choice Irish comrades,
Filled with earnest, calm devotion,
Fridolin sailed o'er the ocean;
Came into the Frankish Empire,
Where at Paris reigned King Clovis.
Smiling spake he to the pilgrims:
"I had never great affection
For the saints and monkish orders;
Since, however, the accursèd
Allemanic lances whistled
Nearer me than I thought pleasant
On the battlefield of Zulpich,
I have changed my mind entirely—
Even kings will pray in danger.
Where you wander I'll protect you,
And unto your special notice
Recommend the Allemanni:
They are stubborn and thick-headed,
They are still most dogged heathen;
Try to make them good and pious."

Farther on the little band went,
To the land of the Helvetians;
There began their serious labour,
And the holy cross was planted
At the foot of snow-clad Säntis,
Planted by the Bodensee.
When descending from the Jura
Fridolinus saw the ruins
Of Augusta Rauracorum—
Roman walls—there still projected
From the rubbish mighty columns
Of the Temple of Serapis.
But the Altar and the Cella
Were o'ergrown with tangled brambles;
And the ox-head of Serapis
Had been built in o'er the stable
By an Allemanic peasant,
Whose forefathers had most likely
Killed the last priest of Serapis.

Seeing this then, Fridolinus
Crossed himself and travelled onward,
By the green banks of the river.
Evening came, and far already
Had the pious man now wandered.
There beheld he, how the river
Flowed in two divided branches;
And in the green waters smiling
Rose before him a small island,

Sack like lying in the river.
(Hence the peasants, who are never
Over squeamish in comparing,
Called the isle Sacconium.)
Evening came; the larks were singing
Fish sprang snapping from the water;
Through the heart of Fridolinus
 Thrilled a thankful pious gladness.
On his knees he sank down praying,
For he recognised the island
As the vision of his dreaming—
And he praised the Lord in Heaven.

Oft, 'tis true, have many of us
Mortals in these modern ages
Also dreamt of tranquil islands,
Where we happily might nestle,
And the weary heart refresh with
Forest calm and Sabbath quiet.
Many also go with ardent
Longing on the journey, but when
Nearing as they hope their island,
Suddenly it fades before them,
As in southern climes the airy
Image of the fay Morgana.

Full of wonder, a wild native
 Sculled the stranger to the island,
 On a raft made of rough pine logs.

Wild the island: limes and alders
In low marshes here were growing;
On the shore with pebbles covered,
Also stood huge ancient willows;
And some scattered huts with thatched roofs.
Here in summer, when the salmon
Are migrating up the river,
Eager fishermen stand waiting
With their long sharp pikes to spear them.
  Unremitting to his labour
Went the saint—soon stood his log-house
On the solid ground erected;
Near the house the cross he planted.
When the bell at dusk of evening
Rang out far, Ave Maria!
And he prayed devoutly kneeling;
From the Rhine vale, many people
Timidly looked at the island.

  Fierce and stubborn were these Almains.
Once the Roman gods they hated;
Now Franconia's God they hated,
Who at Zulpich, like a tempest,
Had o'erthrown their mighty host.
  When the lazy master idly
Took his rest on winter evenings,
And, with eager zest, the women
Set their tongues in busy motion,

And of this and that they gossiped—
How the jug of milk had curdled,
How the hut was struck by lightning,
How a youth was badly injured
By a boar's sharp tusk when hunting—
Then in warning spoke the crafty
Aged Allemanic grandam :
   "No one else have we to blame but
Him who dwells on yonder island—
That old pallid, praying stranger.
Trust ye not, I pray, the new God
Of the Franks, nor false King Clovis !"
   And they feared the pious stranger.
Once, upon the summer solstice,
They all came unto his island,
Drank there—after ancient custom—
Mead from their enormous tankards ;
And they tried to seize the stranger,
But he had gone down the river.
   "We will leave this pallid man, then,
Tokens that we've held our feast here !"
Soon some lighted brands were flying
In the hut of Fridolinus ;
And they sprang rejoicing through the
Flames in singing, "Praised be Woden !"
From the distance gazed with pleasure
The old grandam, and her face shone
Ghastly in the lurid light.

Fridolinus, when returning,
Saw his hut laid waste in ashes;
And he said, then smiling sadly:
"Lord, I thank thee for these trials,
As they but increase my courage."
Then he built anew his dwelling,
And soon found an entrance open
To the rough hearts of his neighbours.
First the children, then the women,
Listened to his gentle language;
And some of the stubborn fellows
Looked approval, when he showed them
How in Erin, his own country,
They could spear the salmon better;
When he sang them ancient legends—
How, upon the Caledonian
Cliffs, had raged a mighty battle
With the Romans; and how Fingal
Overthrew young Caracalla.
Then they said: "A strong and mighty
God has sent this man here to us;
And a good God, for this stranger
Bringeth blessing on our fishing."
And in vain the grandam warned them:
"Trust ye not, I pray, the new God
Of the Franks and false King Clovis!"

Yes, he touched these hearts so rugged
Taught to them the Christian doctrine;

And they understood that giving
Is more blessed than receiving ;
That it was the Son of God who
On the cross for men did suffer.
Hardly had a year passed over—
'Twas Palm-Sunday—when descended,
From the slopes of all the mountains,
A great throng, who then rowed over
To the isle of Fridolinus.
Peacefully there on the island,
Sword, and shield, and axe they laid down ;
And the children gaily gathered
For themselves the willow blossoms
And sweet violets by the river.
From his hut came Fridolinus,
Fully robed in priestly vestments ;
By his side walked his companions
Who had come from distant places :
Gallas from Helvetia ; also
From the Bodensee Columban.
And they led down to the shore then
The great throng of the converted,
And baptised them in the name of
Father, Son, and Holy Ghost.

She alone did not come with them
To the isle of Fridolinus,
She the old and stubborn grandam ;
And she said : " No new gods need I,

As my life is fast declining.
I'm contented with the old ones,
Who to me are kind and gracious,
Who once gave me my dear husband—
My good, noble Siegebert.
When'er Death from here should take me,
I could never hope to find him;
And for him my heart is yearning.
In the woods I must be buried,
Where the mandrake grows 'neath fir-trees
Which with mistletoe are covered.
I don't wish a cross on my grave,
Shall not envy it to others."

On that very day, however,
Fridolin laid the foundations
Of the cloister and the city;
And his work waxed ever greater,
And afar throughout the country
Was the holy man revered.
When again he paid a visit
To King Clovis' court, in Paris,
On his right the king did place him,
And then solemnly donated
The whole island to his cloister,
And, besides, large tracts of country;
Even a great saint became he.
Have ye never heard the legend
Of the court-day, and Count Ursus,
Which the statues o'er the church door

Have preserved e'en to the present?
A great saint, indeed, became he,
And is still the Rhineland's patron.
To this day prevails the custom
That the peasants have their first-born
By the name of Fridli christened.

* * * *

On the sixth of March young Werner
Gaily parted from the glebe-house;
Gratefully he shook the hand of
The good pastor, who sincerely
Wished him a most pleasant journey.
And the old cook was completely
Reconciled unto the stranger;
Bashfully she cast her eyes down
To the ground, while deeply blushing,
When young Werner, out of mischief,
Kissed his hand to her, when leaving.
Barking ran the two St. Bernards
A long distance with our rider.

Bright and warm the sun was shining
On the town of Fridolinus;
Solemn peals afar resounded,
From the organ of the minster,
As young Werner through the gate rode.
Quickly found he first good shelter
For his horse, and then he walked on
To the crowded lively market,

Went up to the old Cathedral,
And he stood with head uncovered
By the portal, where was passing
Then the festive long procession.

   Through the war the precious relics
Of the Saint had been well hidden
In old Laufenburg's strong castle.
They had often in the city
Missed their presence with much sorrow.
Now that peace once more was settled,
They were striving with fresh ardour
To do honour to their saint.
At the head of the procession
Came gay troops of merry children.
But when they too loudly prattled,
Then their old and gray-haired teacher
Pulled them by the ear and scolded:
   " Keep quite still, my little people!
Take great care, for Fridolinus
May be listening to your gabbling.
He, a Saint severe and holy,
Will complain of you in Heaven."
   Twelve young men came next, who bore the
Coffin, rich with gold and silver,
Which enclosed the Saint's remains.
Bearing it they chanted softly:

   Thou who dwellest high in Heaven,

Bless thy people and thy city,
Stretch o'er us thy arms of mercy,
　　Fridolinus, Fridolinus!
Grant us further thy protection;
From all danger mayst thou guard us,
War and pestilence keep from us,
　　Fridolinus, Fridolinus!

Then the Dean and all the Chaplains
Followed after—bearing tapers
Came the youthful Burgomaster,
Came the town's wise Corporation
And the other dignitaries:
Bailiff, Revenue-receiver,
Syndic, Notary, Attorney,
And the old Chief Ranger also.
(He came only for decorum,
For with Mother Church and Saints' Days
He was not upon good footing,
Prayed much rather in the forest.)
E'en the Messenger and Sergeant
Did not then, as was their custom,
Take a morning draught together,
But joined gravely the procession.
Then in dusky Spanish mantles,
Ornamented with white crosses,
Came the great Teutonic Order,
All the Knights and their Commander.
Down the river stood in Beuggen

The Teutonic Order's Castle
Whence at early dawn of morning
All these knights had come on horseback.

   Then came black-robed, grave and aged,
Noble ladies of the Convent,
And in front by the blue standard
Walked the aged Lady Abbess,
And her thoughts were: " Fridolinus,
Though thou art so full of kindness,
One thing thou canst ne'er restore me,
'Tis my youth, so fair and golden.
It was charming fifty years since,
When my cheeks were red like roses,
And when many knights were captured
In the meshes of my glances!
Long have I done penance for this,
And I hope it is forgiven.
Deeply wrinkled is my forehead,
While the cheeks and lips are faded,
And the sunken mouth is toothless."

   Next the train of noble ladies
Came the burghers' comely housewives,
At the end the elder matrons.
Only one in work-day garments
Kept aloof from the procession,
'Twas the hostess from the ancient
Tavern of the "Golden Button;"
So demanded ancient custom.

There—so learn we from the legend—
Stood once in those heathen ages
An old tavern; Fridolinus,
When he first upon the island
Set his foot, had there sought shelter;
But the landlord, a rude heathen,
Spoke unto the holy man thus:
"All you priests are good for nothing,
But to vilify our old gods;
And you seldom carry even
One red farthing in your pocket.
So begone from off my threshold!"
Now the purse of Fridolinus
Had indeed but little in it,
And he had to take his night's rest
Underneath the shady lindens
In the meadow. But the angels
Cared well for him, and he found out,
On awaking, that his purse was
Filled with golden Roman pieces.
Then again the Saint did visit
The inhospitable tavern,
Took a meal, and paid in shining
Money what the host demanded;
And to shame him left moreover
Seven gold coins as a present.
Thus for an eternal warning
To all landlords void of pity,
Although ages had elapsed since,

No one from the "Golden Button"
Could join in the Saint's procession.

As the flowers in the mown field
Gaily bloom 'mid dried up stubble,
So close by the elder matrons
Walked the lovely group of maidens,
Clad in snow-white festive garments.
Many old men, as they saw them
Passing by in youthful beauty,
Thought: "Upon our guard we must be,
For these maidens are as dangerous
As a Swedish regiment."
In the front they bore a statue
Of Our Lady, dress'd most richly,
In a purple velvet garment,
Which they had presented to her,
As a grateful holy offering,
When the weary war was ended.
In that lovely file the fourth one
Was a slender, light-haired maiden;
On her curls, a wreath of violets,
Over which the white veil floated,
And it covered half her features,
Like the hoar-frost in the Spring-time
Glistening on the early rosebud.
With her eyes cast down she passed by
Where young Werner now was standing.
He beheld her. Had the sun then

Blinded suddenly his eyesight,
Or the fair young maiden's beauty?

   Although others still came past him,
Rooted to the spot he stood there,
Looking only at the fourth one,
Gazed, and gazed; when the procession
Turned the corner of a side street
Still he gazed, as if the fourth one
In the file he must discover.
"He is caught!" so goes the saying
In that country, when one's soul is
By the wand of love enchanted;
Love can never be our captive,
We are wholly conquered by him.
So beware, my young friend Werner!
Joy and sorrow hides the saying:
"He is caught!" I need not say more.

FOURTH PART.

YOUNG WERNER'S ADVENTURES ON THE RHINE.

MIRTH now reigned within the city.
Those who early had united
In the honoured Saint's procession,
Now sat, equally united,
Drinking the good wine before them,
Or the golden foaming beer.
Corks were popping, glasses ringing;
Many huge and mighty goblets
By the guests were emptied quickly,
In St. Fridolinus' honour.
Simpering with delight, the landlord
Counted all the empty barrels,
And, with a devout expression,
Chalked them all upon the blackboard.
From the inn outside the gate, which
By the peasants was frequented,
Came gay music; for, with legs crossed,
There sat, playing on his fiddle,

Schwefelhans, the violinist ;
And in wild and boisterous dances
Were the Hauenstein young peasants
Twirling round their buxom partners.
Groaning was the floor, and shaking
'Neath their feet and heavy stamping,
From the walls the plaster falling,
So uproarious was their shouting.
From afar, with turned-up noses,
Many dandies looked on sneering ;
Yet, within themselves were thinking :
" Better, after all, than nothing."

The sedate and older people
Sat together in the tap-room.
As their ancestors delighted
To get drunk in Woden's honour,
So, in true historic spirit,
They for Fridolin got tipsy.
Many troubled faithful consorts
Pulled their husbands by the coat-tail,
When the second and the third piece
Of hard money here was squandered ;
But the husband said quite coolly :
" Dearest wife, control thy humour,
For to-day all must be spent here ! "
And he left not till the watchman
With the halberd came and ordered
That 'twas time to close the tavern.

With uncertain steps, ill-humoured,
To his mountain-home he totters:
And the silent night is witness
Of some sudden headlong tumbles.
But she covers them with darkness—
Kindly—as she does the beating
Which, as finish to the feasting,
He bestows on his poor consort.

    Lonely, far-off from the bustle,
Walked young Werner toward the Rhine-strand,
Without thinking where he wandered.
Still before his eyes there hovered
Those sweet features of the maiden
Which he had beheld that morning,
But now seemed a dream's fair vision.
Burning was his brow; his eyes now
Restlessly strayed up to heaven,
Then he cast them meekly downward,
As if asking where to find her;
And he did not mind the north wind,
Which his locks dishevelled sadly.
Through his heart hot glowing thoughts ran
Wildly chasing one another,
Like the mist, which in the autumn
Moves around the tops of mountains
In most oddly-changing shapes;
And it rang and surged within him,

Like the first germ of a poem
Growing in the mind's recesses.

  Also, thus, in bygone ages,
By the Arno strolled another
Child of man, plunged in deep musing;
And he also blew the trumpet,
Which, like that of the last judgment,
Rang aloud, in piercing notes, through
His benighted rotten age.
But when he, upon that feast-day,
First beheld the wondrous maiden
Who his leading star through life was,
And to Paradise did lead him;
He then wandered by the river,
Under shady oaks and myrtles;
And, for all the joyful feelings
Which within his heart were ringing,
He could only find the utterance:
"Beatricè! Beatricè!"
And thus, after many thousand
And still thousand years have rolled by,
Others, who with love are stricken,
Dreamily will walk the same way.
And whenever the last scion
Of the Germans on the Rhine-shore
Has been gathered to his fathers,
Then will others walk and muse there,

And in gentle foreign language
Murmur the sweet words : " I love thee ! "
Do you know them ?   They have noses
Somewhat flattened out and ugly ;
By the Aral and the Irtish,
Now their ancestors drink whisky,
But to them belongs the future.

   Youthful love, thou pearl so precious,
To the wounded heart a balsam,
To life's tossing ship an anchor,
Oasis in sandy deserts ;
Never would I venture singing
Any new song to thy honour.
I'm one of the Epigoni ;
And great hosts of valiant people
Lived before King Agamemnon.
I know also wise King Solomon,
And the petty German poets.
Bashful only, and most grateful,
I recall thy gentle magic.
As a golden light it shineth
Through the mists of youth, and clearly
To our view unveils life's outlines ;
Shows us where to plant our footsteps,
And gives courage to the wanderer.
Lofty hopes and timid longing,
Dauntless thoughts and stubborn courage,
All these do we owe to Love ;

And the cheerful heart that helps us,
Like a mountain-staff, to spring o'er
Rocks which lie upon our pathway.

Happy, therefore, is the heart which
Love triumphantly has entered!
But young Werner seemed unconscious
Why he thus to-day was strolling
Idly here along the river.
Dreamily he walked close by it,
Heedless of the waves which often
Gave his boots a thorough wetting.

From the river's depths gazed at him
Then the Rhine, who just the battle
Of two aged crabs was watching,
And with noisy, ringing laughter,
Nodded praises, when in rage they
Crossed their horny claws together.
Yes, the Rhine—he is a handsome
Youthful man, and not alone a
Geographical conception—
For young Werner he felt pity.
Rustling rose he from the water,
In his locks a wreath of rushes,
And a reed-staff in his right hand.
Werner, like all Sunday children,
Saw much more than other mortals;

So he quickly recognised him,
And made him a low obeisance.

   Smiling then to him the Rhine said:
"Have no fear, my dear young dreamer,
For I know where thy shoe pinches.
Ye are strange and odd, ye mortals;
Ye believe ye bear a secret
Through the world in lonely musing,
And each chafer understands it;
E'en the gnats and the mosquitoes
See it on your heated foreheads,
See it in your tearful glances,
That Love holds you in his meshes.
Have no fear, I know what love is;
I have heard upon my journeys
Many false and many true vows
Whispered in Romansh and German,
Also in the Low Dutch language
(In the last oft most insipid).
Nightly likewise have I listened
Near the shores to much flirtation
And much kissing, yet kept silent.
Many a poor devil also,
In whose heart deep grief was gnawing,
In my waves found peace and comfort.
When the water-nymphs had gently
Lulled him there to sleep, I bore him
Off with care to shores far distant.

Under willows, under rushes,
Far from tongues of deadly malice,
Rest is sweet to false Love's victims.
Many thus have I so buried;
I have also harboured many
On the river's deep cool bottom
In my crystal water-palace;
Lodged them well so that they never
Longed for man, nor for returning.

Have no fear, I know what love is.
I myself feel something tightening
Round my heart, when I the Schwarzwald's
Mountains greet, and jump rejoicing
O'er Schaffhausen's precipices,
Force my way with courage, rushing
Through the straits of Laufenburg.
For I know that soon my lovely
Schwarzwald child, the youthful Wiese,
Comes to meet me, bashful, timid;
And she prattles, in the rough speech
Of the Almains, of the Feldberg,
Of the ghosts beheld at midnight,
Of sweet mountain flowers, and huge
Caps and thirsty throats at Schopfheim.
Yes, I love her, I have never
Gazed enough at her blue eyes yet.
Yes, I love her, I have never
Kissed enough her rosy cheeks yet.

Oft I rush, like thee, a dreamer,
Wildly past old sober Basel,
Get quite tired of the tedious
Old town-councillors, and ruin
Now and then a wall in passing.
And they think, it was in anger,
What was only done in frolic.
Yes, I love her. Many other
Charming women much pursue me;
None, however,—e'en the stately,
Richly vine-clad, blue-eyed Mosel—
Ever from my heart can banish
Thee, the Feldberg's lovely daughter.
When I through the sands of Holland
Weary drag my sluggish waters,
And I hear the wind-mills clapper,
Tender longings oft steal o'er me
For my early lovely sweetheart.
Then with deep dull sound my waves roll,
Onward through the tedious meadows,
Roll out far into the North Sea,
But not one there understands me.

Have no fear; I know what love is.
Ye I know, ye German dreamers
Who on my fair shores are dwelling.
I, indeed, am your true likeness,
Am the history of your nation;
Storm and passion, bitter ending,

FOURTH PART.

All are pictured in my course.
Most romantic is my birthplace,
And weird Alpine spirits watched well
By my glittering icy cradle,
And conducted me to daylight.
Strong and wild was I in childhood;
Never can the rocks be counted,
Which I roaring dashed to pieces,
And hurled up like balls at tennis.
Fresh and gay I then float onward,
Through the Swabian sea, and carry,
Unimpaired, my youthful powers
Farther to the German country.
And once more come up before me
All the fragrant recollections
Of romance; my youthful dreaming
Sweetly then returns transfigured:
Foam and surging, strong-walled cities,
Rocks and castles, quiet cloisters,
Smiling vineyards on the hillside;
From the tower calls the watchman,
And the pennon gaily flutters,
And from yonder cliff is ringing
Wondrously the Lurley's song.
But, alas! the good time passes;
Nought but grief is then my portion;
I devote myself to drinking,
Pray at Cöln in the Cathedral,
And become a beast of burden.

Shabby tradesmen must I serve then,
On my ill-used back must carry
All the Dutchman's clumsy tow-boats.
In the sand, to me so hateful,
Wearily my way I drag on,
And I've long been dead already,
Ere my grave, the sea, receives me.
So beware of such stagnation!

   Yes, I can much more relate thee;
I to-day am in good humour,
And I love all jovial fellows,
Who like thee and like myself face,
Gaily with light hearts, the Future.
But I'll end this long discourse now,
And will give thee my best counsel.
I know well that thou art love-struck,
Know, thou lovest Margaretta,
The old Baron's lovely daughter,
Whose old castle standing yonder
Is in my green waves reflected.
Oft I see with joy the maiden
Standing there upon the terrace,
And I'll gladly take thee near her.
There's the boat and there's the rudder;
All the rest may well be trusted
To thy own instinctive wisdom."
Saying this, he shook his locks, and
Dived beneath the water's surface;

And the foaming surging waves then
Closed the whirlpool where he vanished.
And afar rang out his laughter,
For, the battle of the crab had
Ended now, one lay there bleeding,
Of the tail bereft the other.

   Werner did as he was counselled.
An old tower was there standing
By the shore, half in the river;
And where through a secret wicket
To the strand came down the fisher,
Was a quiet hidden inlet,
Where lay boat and rudder ready.
As the boatman kept the feast-day,
So without permission Werner
Took possession of the boat there.
In the meantime evening crept on:
Here and there rang from the mountains
Clear and sharp, a shouting from some
Tipsy peasant going homeward.
O'er those distant pine-tree forests
Streamed the moonlight through the valley;
Bashfully some stars already
From the clear blue sky were peeping.
From the shore shoved off young Werner.
As a horse, when in his stable
Long imprisoned, gaily prances,
Neighs with joy, when he can carry

Through the fields again his master:
So shot boldly swiftly downward,
On the water gaily bounding,
The light boat, and speeding onward
Passed the walls of the old city.
Soon it gained the ancient Rhine bridge,
Which with timber-covered arches
Boldly spans from shore to shore.
And courageously young Werner
Steered right through below the third pier,
Laughing, when, as if to vex him,
Three times up and three times downward
Danced his boat, seized by the whirlpool.
Soon he now beheld the castle
With its gable-roofs and turrets,
Shining through the lofty chestnuts,
All illumined by the moonlight.
Yonder rose up from the river
By the shore a bank of gravel,
Bare and barren; it was often
Flooded over by the river.
Out of fun the country people
Called it field of Fridolinus.
Thither now the frail boat drifted;
There it halted on the shelving
Pebbly ground. Out jumped young Werner,
And he looked with eager glances
Whether he could not descry her.
He could only see a distant

FOURTH PART.

Twinkling light up in the turret;
But this wholly satisfied him.
Often doth a distant vision
More delight bestow upon us
Than the fulness of possession;
Hence our Song dwells on his pleasure,
As he stands there on the sand-bank
At that light in rapture gazing.
Spread before his dreamy eyes lay
Rosy visions of the future;
Neither sun nor stars shone in them,
Nothing but that light's faint glimmer.
From the turret, where it flickered,
Love flew forth, on rapid pinions,
Noiselessly to him descended,
And unseen stood there beside him
On the field of Fridolinus;
And he handed him the trumpet
Which from Werner's neck was hanging,
Saying: Blow your trumpet, blow it!

And he blew until his blowing
Filled with melody the night air.
In the depths the Rhine was listening,
Salmon, trout, and pike were listening,
Water-nymphs were listening also,
And the wind the ringing tones bore
To the castle tenderly.

FIFTH PART.

THE BARON AND HIS DAUGHTER.

Now, my Muse, thy powers summon!
For thy path leads to the Baron
And the lovely Margaretta.
Now be circumspect and courteous;
For, an aged trooper-colonel
Might with thee and others like thee
Not be very ceremonious;
But might throw thee down the staircase,
Which is steep and very slippery,
And might prove injurious to thee.
Now, my Muse, mount upward to the
Castle gate, behold there sculptured
The three balls upon the scutcheon,
As in the armorial bearings
Of the Medici in Florence—
Signs of ancient, noble lineage;
Now ascend the steps of sandstone,
Loudly knock at the great hall door,

Then step in and give report of
What thou there hast slyly noticed.
In the spacious, lofty knights' hall,
With its walls of panelled oak-wood,
And with rows of old ancestral
Dusty portraits decorated,
There the Baron took his comfort,
Seated in his easy arm-chair
By the cheerful blazing fire.
His mustache was gray already;
On his forehead, which a Swedish
Trooper's sword had deeply scarred once,
Many wrinkles had been furrowed
Also by the hand of Time.
And a most unpleasant guest had
Taken quarters uninvited
In the left foot of the Baron.
Gout 'tis called in vulgar parlance,
But if any learnèd person
Rather podagra should call it,
I shall offer no objection;
Not the less will be its torments.
Just this day the pangs were milder,
Only now and then increasing,
When the Baron, smiling, spoke thus:

" Zounds! 'tis evident that in the
Long and dreadful Thirty Years' war,
E'en this plaguy gout adopted

Something of the art of tactics.
The attack begins in order ;
First the skirmishers go forward,
Then the flying columns follow.
Oh, I wish the devil had them,
This whole reconnoitring party !
But not even this sufficeth.
Just as if I had a fortress
In my heart—like guns 'tis roaring.
Then it throbs like storming parties,
Piff ! paff ! I capitulate."

But just then there was a truce held.
So the Baron took his comfort
As he filled out of the stone jug
His large goblet brimming over.
Up by Hallau where the last spurs
Of the Hohe-Randen's ridges
To the Rhine are sloping downward,
Where the vintner, while at labour,
Hears the ceaseless mighty roaring
Of the Rhine-fall by Schaffhausen :
Had the sun with fervent glowing
Ripened well the spicy red wine
Which the Baron had selected
As his usual evening beverage.
And, to heighten his enjoyment,
He puffed out clouds of tobacco.
In his red and simple clay-pipe

Burned the weed from foreign countries,
Which he smoked through a long pipe-stem
Made of fragrant cherry-wood.

At the Baron's feet was lying
Gracefully the worthy tom-cat,
Hiddigeigei, with the coal-black
Velvet fur and mighty tail.
'Twas an heirloom from his long-lost,
Much-beloved, and stately consort,
Leonore Monfort du Plessys.
Hiddigeigei's native country
Was Hungaria, and his mother,
Who was of the race Angora,
Bore him to a Puszta tom-cat.
In his early youth to Paris
He was sent as a fond token
Of the love of an Hungarian,
Who, though far in Debreczin, still
With due reverence had remembered
The blue eyes of Leonora,
And the rats in her old palace.
With the stately Leonora
To the Rhine came Hiddigeigei.
A true house-pet, somewhat lonesome
Did he while away his life there ;
For, he hated to consort with
Any of the German cat-tribe.
" They may have," thus he was thinking

In his consequential cat-pride,
"Right good hearts, and may possess too
At the bottom some good feeling,
But 'tis polish that is wanting;
A fine culture and high breeding,
I miss sorely in these vulgar
Natives of this forest-city.
And a cat who won his knight spurs
In fair Paris, and who often
In the quarter of Montfaucon
Has enjoyed a racy rat-hunt,
Misses in this little town here
All that is to him congenial,
Any intercourse with equals."
Isolated, therefore, but still
Ever dignified and solemn
Lived he in this lonely castle.
Graceful through the halls he glided,
Most melodious was his purring;
And in fits of passion even,
When he curved his back in anger,
And his hair stood bristling backward,
Never did he fail to mingle
Dignity with graceful bearing.
But when over roof and gable
Up he softly clambered, starting
On a hunting expedition,
Then mysteriously by moonlight
His green eyes like emeralds glistened;

Then, indeed, he looked imposing
This majestic Hiddigeigei.

  Near his cat sat the old Baron.
In his eyes were often flashes,
Now like lightning—then more softened
Like the mellow rays of sunset,
As he thought of bygone times.
To old age belongs the solace
Of recalling days of yore.
Thus the aged ne'er are lonely.
The dear shades are floating round them,
Of the dead, in quaint old garments,
Gorgeous once, now sadly faded.
But fond memory blots decay out,
And the skulls once more with beauty
Are arrayed in youthful freshness.
Then they talk of days long vanished,
And the aged heart is beating,
And the fist oft clinches tightly.
  As he passes by her turret,
Once again she smiling greets him;
Once again resound the trumpets,
And the fiery charger bears him
Neighing to the throng of battle.

  So the Baron with good humour
Of the Past review was holding—
And, when oft he stretched his hand out,

Suddenly grasped at his goblet,
And a deep long draught then swallowed:
Probably a dear and lovely
Vision rose up bright before him.
Oft it seemed as if his memory
Clung to things which gave less pleasure;
For sometimes, without a reason,
Down there came on Hiddigeigei's
Back a kick with cruel rudeness.
And the cat thought it more prudent
Then his resting-place to alter.

   Now into the hall stepped lightly
The old Baron's lovely daughter
Margaretta,—and her father
Nodded kindly as she entered.
Hiddigeigei's suffering face too
Showed delight as cats express it.
She had changed her festal white robe
For a garment of black velvet.
On her long and golden tresses,
A black cap sat most coquettish,
'Neath which her blue eyes were smiling
With a matron-like expression;
To the girdle was attached the
Bunch of keys and leather-pocket,
German housewife's badge of honour.
And she kissed the Baron's forehead,
Saying: " Dear papa, don't blame me,

If to-day I kept you waiting.
The old Lady Abbess yonder
In the convent did detain me,
Told me many things of import,
Wisely of old age discoursing,
And of Time, the great destroyer.
The Commander too of Beuggen
Said such sweet things, just as if they
Came right from the comfit-maker.
I was glad, when I could leave them.
For your lordship's further pleasure
Here I am, all due attention.
I am ready, from your favourite
Theuerdank to read aloud now;
For, I know, you like the rougher
Tales of hunting and adventure,
Better than the mawkish sweetness
Of our present pastoral poets.

"But, O wherefore, dearest father,
Are you ever, ever smoking
This bad poisonous tobacco?
I am frightened when I see you
Sitting there in clouds enveloped
As in times of fog the Eggberg.
And I'm sorry for the gilded
Picture-frames hung on the walls there,
And the pretty snow-white curtains.
Don't you hear their low complaining,

How the smoke from your red-clay pipe
Makes them faded, gray and rusty?
'Tis most truly a fine country,
That America which once the
Spanish admiral discovered.
I myself take great delight in
The gay plumage of the parrots,
And the pink and scarlet corals;
Dream at times also of lofty
Graceful palm-groves, lonely log-huts,
Cocoa-nuts, gigantic flowers,
And of mischievous wild monkeys.
I wish almost it were lying
In the sea still undiscovered;
All because of this tobacco
Which has been imported hither.
I can grant a man forgiveness,
Who more often than is needed
Draws his red wine from the barrel,
And could get, if necessary,
Reconciled unto his red nose;
Never to this horrid smoking."

Smiling had the Baron listened,
Smiling he puffed many smoke-clouds
From his clay-pipe, and then answered:
" Dearest child, you women always
Thoughtlessly do talk of many
Things beyond your comprehension.

It is true that soldiers often
Take up many evil habits,
Not adapted to the boudoir.
But my daughter finds with smoking
Too much fault; for through this habit
I have won my wife and household.
And because to-day so many
Old campaign tales through my head run,
Do not read to-night. Sit down here;
I will now relate thee something
Of this much-abused tobacco,
And of thy blest angel mother."

   Sceptically, Margaretta
With her large blue eyes looked at him,
Took her work up to embroider,
Coloured worsted and her needle,
Moved her stool then near the Baron's
Arm-chair, and sat down beside him.
Charming picture! In the forest,
Round the knotty oak thus climbeth
The wild rose in youthful beauty.
Then the Baron at one swallow
Drank his wine, and thus related:

   " When the wicked war was raging,
I once roved with some few German
Troopers yonder in fair Alsace;
Hans von Weerth was our good colonel.

Swedes and French laid siege to Breisach,
And their camp was all alive with
Stories of our daring ventures.
But who e'er can stand 'gainst numbers?
So one day the hounds attacked us,
Just as if wild beasts they hunted;
And at last, when bleeding freely
From the wounds their fangs inflicted,
We were forced to lay our arms down.
Afterwards the French transported
Us as prisoners to Paris,
Caged us in Vincennes' strong fortress.
'Damn them!' said our valiant colonel,
Hans von Weerth, 'it was much nicer,
Galloping, with shining sabres
Hostile lines to charge with fury,
Than on this hard bench to sit here,
And to battle with ennui thus.
For this foe there is no weapon,
Neither wine nor even dice-box,
Nothing but tobacco. I once
Tried it in the country of the
Dull Mynheers, and here it also
Will do service; let us smoke then!'
    The commander of the fortress
Got a keg of best Varinas
For us from a Dutch retailer,
Got us also well-burnt clay-pipes.
In the prisoners' room commenced now

FIFTH PART.

Such a smoking, such a puffing
Of dense clouds of strong tobacco
As no mortal eyes had seen yet
In the gallant Frenchmen's country.
Full of wonder gazed our jailors,
And the news spread to the king's ears,
And the king himself in person
Came to see this latest marvel.
Soon all Paris rang with stories
Of the wild and boorish Germans,
And of their, as yet unheard of,
Truly wondrous feats in smoking.
Coaches drove up, pages sprang down,
All came to the narrow guard-room,
Cavaliers and stately ladies;
She came also, she the noble
Leonore Montfort du Plessys.
Even now I see her slight foot
Stepping on our rough bare stone-floor,
Hear her satin train still rustling,
And my soldier's heart is beating
As if in the thick of battle.
Like the smoke from the big cannons
Came the smoke out of my clay-pipe;
And 'twas well so. On the same cloud
Which I puffed there in the presence
Of the proud one, sat god Cupid,
Gaily shooting off his arrows,
And he knew well how to hit right.

Out of wonder grew deep interest,
Then the interest fast to love changed,
And the German bear appeared soon
Finer far and nobler than the
Paris lions altogether.

"When, at last, the gates were opened
Of our dungeon, and the herald
Brought us tidings of our freedom,
I was then still more a captive
Bound in Leonora's fetters;
And remained thus, and the wedding
Which soon took us home to Rhine-land
Only made the rivets stronger.
When I think of this, I feel that
Tears on my mustache are rolling.
For what now to me remaineth
Of the past so fair, but memory,
And the black cat, Hiddigeigei,
And my Leonora's image,
Thou my child. God give her soul rest!"

Speaking thus, he knocked the ashes
From his pipe, and patted gently
Hiddigeigei; but his daughter
Roguishly knelt down before him,
Saying: " Dearest father, grant me
Your entire absolution.
Never shall you hear in future

From my lips an observation
On account of this vile smoking."

    Graciously the Baron said then:
"Thou hast also been sarcastic
At my drinking oft too freely;
And I have a mind to tell thee
Still a most instructive story,
How in Rheinau in the cloister,
As the guest of the Lord Abbot
I went through a bout of drinking
In the famous wine of Hallau.
But"——the Baron stopped and listened.
"Zounds!" he said, "what's that I hear there?
Whence doth come that trumpet-blowing?"
Werner's music through the March night,
Plaintive soared up to the castle,
Begging entrance like a pet-dove,
Which, returning to its mistress,
Finds the window closed and fastened,
And begins to peck and hammer.
To the terrace went the Baron
And his daughter; Hiddigeigei
Followed both with step majestic.
Through the cat's heart then swept omens
Of a great, eventful future.
All around they looked—but vainly.
For the turret's gloomy shadow
Covered both the bank and Werner.

Like the blowing of the moot, then
Like the clanging charge of horsemen,
Up it mounted to the terrace,
Then died out ;—a small boat dimly
They saw moving up the river.

Backward stepped the Baron quickly,
Pulled the bell and called his servant
Anton, who came in directly.
"Gain immediate information
Who was blowing here the trumpet
On the Rhine at this late hour.
If a spirit, sign the cross thrice ;
If a mortal, greet him kindly,
And command his presence hither,
For with him I must hold converse."
Soldier-like, saluting, turned then
Right about face good old Anton :
"I'll fulfil your lordship's orders."

Meanwhile, silently descended
Midnight over vale and city ;
And in Margaretta's slumbers
Came a dream most sweet and wondrous:
As she walked to the old minster
Once again in festal garments,
Fridolinus came to meet her ;
By his side there walked another,
But 'twas not the dead man who once

FIFTH PART.

Followed him to Glarus court-house;
'Twas a youth, fair, tall, and slender;
Like a trumpeter he looked, and
Greeted her with lowly reverence;
While Saint Fridolin was smiling.

SIXTH PART.

HOW YOUNG WERNER BECAME THE BARON'S TRUMPETER.

Master Anton started early
The next morning for the city,
To find out that trumpet blower.
By St. Fridolin's cathedral
He turned off into a side-street.
From the other side there came with
Rapid steps the boatman Martin,
And they met just at the corner,
Bumping up against each other.
"'Pon my soul," cried out the worthy
Anton, as he rubbed his forehead;
"Your thick skull is hard as iron."
"Yours is not upholstered either
With soft wool or springy sea-weed,"
Was the boatman's ready answer.
"And what business have you running
Through the city's streets thus early?"
"I can ask the same," said Anton.

"I seek someone who last evening
From the shore my boat unfastened,"
Answered him the boatman Martin.
" He may be my man," said Anton.
" When I came down to the river,
There I found my boat turned over
On the shore—the rudder broken,
And the fastening cut asunder.
If a thunderstorm would only
Sweep away these wicked people,
Who like thieves at night are roving
On the Rhine in borrowed vessels."
" And the trumpet blow," said Anton.—
" But whenever I shall find him,
To the justice I shall take him.
He must pay me; even for the
Black and blue mark which you gave me,
I shall bring a heavy reckoning.
It is shameful how this fellow
Gives me such vexation!" Thus the
Boatman scolding went on farther.

" And I do not see myself, why
I should take such extra trouble
To hunt up this mischief-maker,"
Said old Anton to himself then.
" Seems to me it is already
Just the time when honest people
For their morning draught are longing."

To the "Golden Button's" shady
Tap-room turned the worthy Anton
Now his steps, and through a side-door
In he stepped: he deemed it wiser
Thus to hide before the public
Such an early morning visit.
Many worthy folks already
Had there quietly assembled
O'er their brimming foaming bumpers.
Like red roses shone their faces,
And like radishes their noses.
"Want a big glass?" asked the waitress
Our old Anton, who assented:
"To be sure! hot is the weather,
And when I woke up, already
In my throat I felt a dryness."
So good Anton soon was drinking
From his large Bohemian bumper,
Turning over in his mind well,
How he should despatch his business.

In the private room was sitting,
Just then Werner with the landlord,
Who had served for his guest's breakfast
A fine slice of red smoked salmon,
And commenced with the young stranger
An instructive conversation:
On the vintage in the Rhine-Pfalz,
How the price of hops was standing,

SIXTH PART.

How they fared in time of war there.
Now and then, to sound the stranger,
He threw slyly out some questions,
Whence he came and what his business.
Still he gained no satisfaction;
But quite shrewdly thus he reasoned:

" He's no bookworm, for he seemeth
Much too martial—nor a soldier
Either, as he looks too modest;
He may be a necromancer,
An adept in all dark witchcraft,
Alchemy, and other black arts.
Wait, I'll catch thee;" and he turned their
Talk to hidden buried treasures,
And to midnight exorcisms.
" Yes, my friend, here near the city
Lies a sandbank in the river.
At the time of Fridolinus
Heaps of gold coin there were buried.
One who knows, a clever fellow,
Could there dig and make his fortune."

" I already saw the sandbank,"
Said young Werner, " when I rowed there
On the Rhine last night by moonlight."

" What, you know it then already?"
Said the landlord much astonished.

"Have I caught thee?" he thought, keenly
Looking at young Werner's pockets,
If he could not hear a jingling
Of great lots of golden money.

"Have I caught thee?" also gladly
To himself said worthy Anton.
"It is, after all, the right thing
Thus to take an early potion."
From the spot where he was seated
He had heard their conversation;
And besides upon the table,
By the stranger's sword and cocked hat,
Also lay the sought-for trumpet.
Drawing near, then, he said gravely:

"With your leave, if you're no spirit—
And that seems to me unlikely,
As you've just enjoyed your breakfast—
Then the Baron sends you greeting,
And invites you to his castle.
I will take you there with pleasure."
Thus he spoke. Young Werner listened,
Half astonished, and went with him.

Smirking, thought the cunning landlord:
"You will get it, my young master;
You believed you had full freedom
Thus to rove about the river,

Spying out long-buried treasures.
But the Baron found you out soon,
And will stop your bold proceedings.
Now you'll get it, when he treats you,
From his amply-furnished stores, to
Some of his well-seasoned curses.
Like a top your head will spin then,
And your ears buzz like a beehive.
But this will concern you solely.
If he keep you in a dungeon
Of your horse I'll take possession ;
It will well score off your reckoning."

Once more in the hall together
Were the Baron and his daughter,
And again he smoked his pipe there,
When the ponderous folding-doors were
Opened, and, with modest reverence,
Werner entered. "If you only,"
Said the faithful Anton, " only
Knew, your gracious lordship, what a
Heavy task it was to find him!"
Keenly did the Baron's eyes rest
On young Werner, passing muster ;
By her father, lightly leaning
On his arm-chair, Margaretta
Bashfully looked at the stranger,
And with both the first impression
Of each other was most happy.

"It is you, then," said the Baron,
"Who last night have startled us here
With your trumpet-blowing, therefore
I should like to speak to you now."
"This commences well," thought Werner,
And, embarrassed, cast his eyes down
To the ground. But the old Baron,
Kindly smiling, thus continued :
"You believe, perhaps, I shall now
Call you to account for having
Made loud music near the castle?
You are wrong, 'tis not my business;
For no license is here needed
On the Rhine; if anybody
Wants to catch a cold by playing
Late at night there, he may do so.
No, I only wish to ask you,
Whether you would like here often
As last night to blow the trumpet?
But I fear I am mistaken.
You are not by trade a player,
May be one of those damned scribblers,
Secretary to a foreign
Embassy, as many are now
Coaching all about the country,
Just to spoil all that the soldier's
Ready sword had once accomplished?"
"Not bad either," thought young Werner;
Still he liked the Baron's manner.

SIXTH PART.

"I am no professional player,"
Said he, "and still less a scribbler.
As for my part, all the inkstands
In the Holy Roman Empire
Might dry up without my caring.
I am not in any service,
But as my own lord and master
I am travelling for my pleasure,
And await whatever fortune
On my pathway may be blooming."

"Very good, then," said the Baron.
"If it stands thus, you may well hear
Everything I have to tell you ;
But before we go on farther,
With old wine it must be seasoned."
Cleverly his thoughts divining,
Margaretta, from the cellar,
Now brought up two dusty bottles
Which, with spider-webs all covered,
In the sand had lain half-buried ;
Brought with them two fine-cut goblets,
Which she filled and then presented.
"This wine ripened long before the
War raged in our German country,"
Said the Baron. "'Tis a famous
Choice old wine which grew at Grenzach.
Brightly in the glass it sparkles,
Like pure gold its colour shineth,

And a fragrance rises from it
Like the finest greenhouse flowers.
Master Trumpeter, ring glasses!"

Loudly then rang both their goblets.
Emptying his, the Baron spun out
Farther still the conversation.
"My young friend, you know, as long as
This world lasts, there will be people
Who are fond of hobby-horses.
Some are mystics and ascetics,
Others love old wine or brandy.
Some, antiquities are seeking,
Others are for chafers craving;
Many others make bad verses.
'Tis a curious joke that each one
Much prefers to choose a calling
Most unsuited to his nature.
I thus also ride my hobby,
And this hobby is the noble
Muse of music who regales me.
As King Saul's deep sorrow vanished
At the sound of David's harp once,
So with cheering sounds of music
Do I banish age's inroads
And the gout, my old disturber.
When sometimes in *tempo presto*
I an orchestra am leading,
Oft I think I'm once more riding

At the head of my brave squadrons.
Right wing, charge the enemy! charge!
At them now you piercing violins!
Fire away you kettle-drums now!
In the town here there are many
Skilful players—though among them
Is a want of sense artistic,
And of connoisseurship, only
Their good will doth hide their failings.
Violin, flute, also viol,
All these parts are well supported
And the contrabass is perfect.
But *one* player still is wanting;
And, my friend, what is a general
Without orderlies, without a
Fugleman the line of battle,
And a band without the trumpet?

"Once 'twas different. These old walls can
Hear him still, the valiant Rassmann,
The chief trumpeter of my squadrons.
Ha! that was a noble blowing!
Rassmann, wherefore didst thou die?

"Still as clear as on his last day,
Do I see him at the shooting
Festival at Laufenburg.
His mustache was fiercely twisted,
Bright and glistening was his trumpet,

And his riding-boots were shining
Like a mirror; I was chuckling.
' 'Tis a point of honour,' said he.
' I must all these Swiss astonish
With myself and with my trumpet.'

' Clear and cheerful rang out yonder
Bugle-horns and trumpets; but as
O'er the choir of forest singers
Sounds the nightingale's sweet warbling,
So above all rang out loudly
Rassmann's wondrous trumpet-blowing.
When we met, his cheeks were scarlet,
And fatigued appeared his breathing.
' 'Tis a point of honour,' said he;
And blew on still. Then were silenced
All the trumpeters from Frickthal,
Those from Solothurn and Aarau,
By the trumpeter great Rassmann.
Once again we met, 'twas evening.
In the ' Golden Swan ' he sat then;
Like a giant 'mid the pigmies
Looked he in this crowd of players.
Many were the goblets emptied
By the trumpeters from Frickthal,
And from Solothurn and Aarau,
But the most capacious goblet
Was drank out by my brave Rassmann.
And with fiery Castelberger,

Which grows on the Aar by Schinznach,
He at last filled up his trumpet.
' 'Tis a point of honour,' said he ;
Drank it out at one long swallow.
' To your health my worthy colleagues !
Thus drinks trumpet-blower Rassmann.'
Midnight had already passed by,
Under tables lay some snoring,
But with steady step and upright
Started Rassmann from the tavern.
On the Rhine with mocking humour
He poured forth a roguish tune yet,
Then a misstep ! Poor, poor Rassmann !
Straight he fell into the river,
And the Rhine's tremendous whirlpool
Thundered foaming and engulfed him,
Him the bravest trumpet-blower.
Ha ! that was a noble blowing !
Rassmann, wherefore didst thou die ? "

    Deeply moved the Baron told this ;
Then continued after pausing :
" My young friend, and think, last evening
On the Rhine a trumpet rang out
Like a greeting from his spirit,
And a tune I heard performed there,
Such a wilderness of sounds, and
Played in Rassmann's finest manner.
If we only had that trumpet,

Then the gap would be filled up well.
And once more I'd lead a full band,
As it were to frays of music.
Therefore hear now my proposal:
Stay with us here in my castle.
Paralysed is now the music
In the forest-city, blow then
New life into her old bones."

Thoughtfully spoke then young Werner:
" Noble lord, you do me honour,
But I nourish a misgiving.
Slim and straight have I thus grown up,
Have not learnt the art of bending
My proud back in any service."

Said the Baron: " Take no trouble
On that head ; because the service
Of the arts enslaves nobody.
Only want of understanding
Makes one lose one's independence.
Be assured, nought is required
Of you but some merry music.
Only, if in idle moments
You would write for me a letter,
Or with my accounts would help me,
I should thank you ; for an ancient
Soldier finds the pen a burden."

Still young Werner hesitated;
But a glance at Margaretta,
And the clouds of doubt all vanished.
" Noble lord," he said, " I'll stay then,
On the Rhine shall be my home now!"
" Bravo!" said the Baron kindly.
" From the prompting of the moment
Have the best results proceeded;
Evil springs from hesitation.
Master Trumpeter ring glasses!
With the golden wine of Grenzach,
With a hearty grasp of hands thus
Let us seal our new-made contract."
Turning then to Margaretta:
" I present to you, my daughter,
This new member of our household."
Then young Werner's silent greeting
Was returned by Margaretta.

" Follow me now through the castle,
My young friend, that I may show you
Where you will abide in future.
In the tower there I have the
Very room for a musician,
O'er the Rhine and mountains looking:
And the radiant morning sun will
Wake you early from your slumber.
There you cosily can nestle,
And the trumpet will sound well there."

From the hall they both proceeded.
From the hall the Baron's daughter
Also went, and in the garden
Gathered cowslips and sweet violets,
Also other fragrant flowers,
Speaking to herself: "How lonely
Must the young man feel here, coming
Thus to dwell with utter strangers!
And, besides, the tower-room looks
With its whitewashed walls so naked,
That I think my pretty nosegay
Will do much for its adornment."

SEVENTH PART.

THE EXCURSION TO THE MOUNTAIN LAKE.

Azure heavens, glowing sunlight,
Bees' low humming, larks' gay carols,
Clear as glass the Rhine's green waters.
On the mountains snow is melting,
In the valleys blossom fruit trees,
May begins his reign at last.

In the path before the hall door
Hiddigeigei took his comfort,
Caring only that the sun's rays
On his fur should fall and warm him.
Through the garden walked the Baron
With his daughter, and with pleasure
He beheld the trees in blossom.
" If my life should be preserved still
For a hundred years or longer,
I should always be delighted
With this wonder-breathing May-time.

True, indeed, I set no value
On the May-dew, though the women
Like to wet with it their faces.
I have never seen a soul yet
Who by it improved her beauty;
Have no faith in arts of witchcraft
In the night of St. Walpurgis,
Nor in broomstick-riding squadrons.
Notwithstanding there belongs a
Magic to the month of May.
My old weary bones have suffered
Many painful gouty twinges
From the chilly winds of April.
Now these pains are quite forgotten,
And I feel as if the old strength
Of my youth were through me streaming,
And as if I were once more a
Beardless trim and gay young ensign,
In those days when at Noerdlingen
I fought fiercely, in close combat
With those brave blue Swedish horsemen.
So I think, it would be pleasant
To agree, this is a feast-day,
Though no Saint has ever claimed it.
Let us saunter through the forest.
I will breathe the balmy pine air,
And the young folks may try whether
Fortune favours them at fishing.

SEVENTH PART.

Yes, to-day I yearn for pleasure.
Anton, get the horses ready."

So 'twas done as he had ordered.
In the court, filled with impatience,
Pawed and neighed the fiery horses.
Full of joyful expectation
For the sport were the young people.
Bent on fishing they had carried
The great net up from the river.
Worthy Anton had invited
Many friends of the old Baron,
Also had communicated
With the ladies of the convent;
And, besides, some uninvited
Guests had also here assembled.
When the landlord of the " Button"
Heard the news, he to his wife said :
"To thy care I trust entirely
All the business of the tavern ;
In thy hands I lay the keys now
Of the cellar and the larder,
I must join the fishing-party."
Speaking thus he stole off quickly ;
Ne'er he missed a hunt or fishing.

Strong and hearty looked the Baron,
On his charger firmly seated

Like a bronze equestrian statue.
By his side on her white palfrey
Rode the lovely Margaretta.
Gracefully to her slim figure
Clung in folds her riding-habit;
Gracefully the blue veil floated
From her riding-hat of velvet.
With a steady hand she boldly
Reined her palfrey, who was bearing
With delight so fair a burden.
Watchfully good Anton followed
His fair mistress; also Werner
After them was gaily trotting,
Though at a respectful distance.
For, behind, in solemn grandeur,
Came the big old-fashioned carriage
Of the Lady Princess Abbess,
With three ladies of the convent,
Likewise old and venerable.
They by Werner were escorted.
He made many courtly speeches
To these old and noble ladies,
And broke many flowering branches
From the trees, and most politely
Handed them into the carriage;
So that, struck with his fine manners,
They unto each other whispered:
"What a pity he's not noble!"

SEVENTH PART.

Up hill steep the road ascended,
And the forest of dark pine-trees
Now received the long procession.
Soon then through the dusky branches
Silver like the mountain-lake shone,
And already merry shouting
Came from thence; for the young people
Of the town had gained the lake-shore
By a shorter steeper path.
At the summit, where the main-road
Took a different direction,
Carriages and riders halted,
And the vehicles and horses
To the servants' care were left.
Full of vigour, through the forest,
Down the hill-slope walked the Baron,
And the ladies followed bravely.
Mosses like the softest velvet
Thickly covered all the ground there,
And descending was not dangerous.
On a ridge, which wide and sunny,
Far into the lake protruded,
Numerous blocks of rock lay scattered.
There the Baron rested, and the
Ladies followed his example.

Deep green lake, dense shade of fir-trees,
Many thousand times I greet you.
I who now this song am singing

Of the past, rejoice in you still.
Oh, how oft ye have refreshed me,
When escaping from the daily
Narrowness of petty town life,
Out to you I used to wander.
Often on the rock I've rested,
Which the roots of the old pine-trees
Cling to, while beneath the lake lies
With its gently rippled surface.
In deep shade the shores lie buried,
But the glittering rays of sunlight
Gaily dance across the water.
All around reigned holy silence,
Only heard there was the hammering
Of the pecker on the pine-trees.
Through the fallen leaves and mosses
Rustled softly emerald lizards,
And with clever questioning glances
Curiously they eyed the stranger.

Yes, I often lay there dreaming;
And when often still at night-fall
I sat there, I heard a rustling
Through the reeds, the water-lilies
Whispered softly to each other.
Then arose from the deep water
Mermaids, whose fair pallid faces
Brightly shone in the soft moonlight.
Heart o'erwhelming, mind bewildering,
Were their gliding graceful motions;

And they beckoned me to come there.
But the fir-tree held and warned me:
"Stay thou here on terra firma,
Hast no business in the water."

   Deep green lake, dense shade of fir-trees,
Oft I think of you quite sadly.
Since those days I've been a wanderer:
I have climbed up many mountains,
And through many lands have travelled,
Looked upon the restless ocean,
And have heard the Sirens singing;
But yet often through my memory
Steal the lake's sweet soothing murmurs,
And soft whispers from the fir-trees,
Home, and love, and youth recalling.

   Now there was a noisy thronging,
Running, shouting, laughing, joking,
Down beneath there on the shore.
Like a general, stood the cunning,
Skilful landlord of the " Button,"
'Mid the crowd of younger people,
And on every side was giving
His wise counsels, how they might now
Have a good successful fishing.
There behind the rocks a boat lay
In the reeds with brushwood covered,
And with chains securely fastened,
That no poachers should disturb it,
Who might come along at midnight,

And employ it for their fishing.
From its hiding-place they dragged it
Onward to the lake-shore, and there
Placed the heavy net within it.
Closely netted were the meshes
Of the coarsest twine, while many
Leaden weights thereon were fastened.
When they tried the boat for leakage,
Although somewhat out of order,
They pronounced it quite seaworthy.

Now the landlord and five comrades,
Gay and hopeful, took their places,
And one end of the great net threw
To some friends on shore remaining,
With the charge to hold it tightly.
From the shore they pushed away now,
Rowing stoutly as the net sank
Slowly down in a wide curve;
Then returned with speed much lessened,
Always dragging on the heavy
Bulky net, so that the fishes
Might therein become entangled.
On the shore they sprang out quickly,
And drew after them the netting,
Till they nigh approached those friends who
Still upon the shore were waiting.
Stoutly pulling back the ends, they
Raised the net out of the water,
In great hopes of lots of booty.

But within itself entangled
It came slowly to the surface
Empty : some unskilful rower
Had prevented it from sinking,
And the dwellers of the lake laughed
To have just escaped such danger.

   Now the landlord cast sharp glances
Over all the meshes. Nothing
Met his anxious gaze but water ;
Not the smallest fish was caught there ;
Only an old boot half rotten,
And a toad half crushed and flattened,
Which with eyes protruding oddly
Looked upon the sunlit forest,
And the human faces round him,
And he thought : " It is most truly
Wonderful, how anybody
Ever can enjoy existence,
With this sky and this bright sunlight !
Well, it seems to me no one here
E'er can have the slightest notion
Of the mud and all its splendour.
Would I were in my own element !"

   Those who stood upon the lake-shore
Raised a long and roaring laughter
At these first-fruits of the fishing.
But in rage broke out the landlord,
O'er their laughter rang his scolding :

"Stupid fellows, bunglers, numskulls!"
And with angry kicks he sent then
All the booty flying swiftly,
Boot and toad in peace together
To the water where they came from.
Loudly splashing they sank downward.

But the disappointed fishers
Would again now try their fortune,
Loosened all the tangled meshes,
And with greatest care they lowered
Then the net and raised it slowly.
And to do so there were needed
Many sturdy pulls and struggles.
Ringing shouts and cries of triumph
Greeted this successful fishing.
From the rock came down the Baron
To the fishers, and the ladies
Eagerly made haste to follow.
Over rocks and thorny brambles
To the shore they found a pathway.
Margaretta followed also,
Notwithstanding her long habit.
When young Werner saw her coming,
Bashfully his arm he offered,
And bewildered were his senses.
So Sir Walter Raleigh's heart once
Must have beaten, when his mantle
He made use of as a carpet

SEVENTH PART.

For his gracious royal mistress.
Yet with thanks fair Margaretta
Werner's arm and aid accepted.
Out there in the verdant forest
Many useless scruples vanish,
Which oft elsewhere greatly trouble
Masters of the ceremonies.
The descent there was not easy,
And no other arm was near her.

By the lake they gaily looked now
At the fishing booty struggling.
Flapping in the net's strong meshes
Were the captives. Many snapping
Sought a way still for escaping,
But on the bare sand were landed ;
And thus fruitless was their trial.
Those who felt toward each other
In the depths such bitter hatred,
Now as captives were quite peaceful :
Snake-like eels, so smooth and slippery,
Well-fed carps with huge broad noses,
And the pirate-fish, the slender
Pike with jaws large and voracious.
As in war, the harmless peasants
Often to stray shots fall victims,
So the fate of being captured
Many others overtook :
Handsome barbels, spotted gudgeons ;

Tiny bleaks, the river-swallow;
And through all this crowd of fishes
Sluggishly the crab was creeping;
Inwardly he sadly grumbled:
"Caught together, hung together."

Well contented said the Baron:
"After labour comes amusement.
Seems to me, that our fresh booty
Will taste better in the forest.
Therefore let us now make ready
For ourselves a rustic dinner."
To these words they all assented,
And the landlord of the "Button"
Sent out two fleet-footed fellows
To the city with the order:
"Two large pans bring quickly hither;
Bring me golden fresh-made butter,
Also bread, and salt sufficient,
And a keg of fine old wine.
Bring me lemons too, and sugar;
For I feel a premonition
As if May-drink would be wanted."
Off they started. Under shelter
Of a rock with a tall pine-tree,
Some the hearth were getting ready,
Bringing there dry boughs and fagots,
Loads of furze and moss together.
Others now prepared the fishes

For the feast, and all the ladies
Gathered herbs of spicy fragrance,
Such as thyme and leaves of strawberries;
Also gathered for the May-wine
The white-blooming fragrant woodroof,
Which rejoiced at being broken
By such tender hands, and thought thus:
"Sweet it was in these dark pine-woods,
To be blooming, 'mid the rocks here,
But still sweeter in the May-time
'Tis to die, and with the last breath
Highly then to spice the May-wine
For the joy of human beings.
Death in general is corruption,
But the woodroof's death is like that
Of the morning-dew on blossoms,
Sweetly, without sighs, exhaling."
From the town returning quickly
Came the two fleet-footed fellows,
Bringing stores, as had been ordered.
And soon crackled on the stone-hearth
Cheerfully a blazing fire.
In the pans were frying briskly
What had recently been swimming.

 First a mighty pike was served up
To the ladies by the landlord,
As a show of rustic cooking;
And a solemn earnest silence
Soon gave evidence that all were

Very busy with the banquet.
Only the confused low sounds of
Gnawing fish-bones, munching crab-claws,
Now disturbed the forest quiet.

  Meanwhile, farther up, delicious
Fragrant May-wine was preparing.
In a bowl of size capacious
Margaretta's taste artistic
Well had brewed it; mild and spicy,
As sweet May himself the drink was.
Every glass she filled up, kindly
Helping all with graceful bearing.
Everybody got his share, and
All were merry round the fire.

  There the city-teacher also
Stretched himself upon the grass-bank.
From the school he had absconded,
Also to enjoy the fishing.
In his heart he bore a secret,
Had to-day composed a song.
May-wine, May-wine, drink of magic!
Suddenly his cheeks were glowing,
And his eyes were shining brightly.
On the rock he sprang courageous,
Saying: "I will sing you something."
Smiling now, the others listened,
And young Werner stepping forward,

On his trumpet low and softly
Blew a piece first as a prelude.
Then upon the rock the teacher
Raised his voice and sang with fervour.
Werner joined him on the trumpet
Clear and joyful, and the chorus
Also fell in—clear and joyful
Through the forest rang the

MAY SONG.

" A wondrous youth of lovely mien
    Rich gifts of joy is strewing ;
O'er hill and vale, where'er are seen
    His footsteps, light is glowing.
        The fresh young green decks hill and lea,
        The birds are singing merrily,
        While falls in gentle showers
        A rain of snow-white flowers.
So in the woods we sing and shout,
    Heigh-tralala loud ringing ;
We sing, while all things bud and sprout,
    To May our welcome bringing.

" Young May in humming sounds delights,
    Is full of merry capers ;
So through the fir-trees swarm great flights
    Of golden buzzing chafers.

And from the moss white lilies rise,
    Of spring the fairest sweetest prize;
    Their bells in tuneful measure
    Ring in the May with pleasure.
So in the woods we sing and shout,
    Heigh-tralala loud ringing;
We sing, while all things bud and sprout,
    To May our welcome bringing.

"Now everyone may think, who can,
    Of mirth, and love that burneth;
To many an old and worthy man
    His youth again returneth.
        His shouts resound across the Rhine:
        'O let me in, thou sweetheart mine!'
        And voices loud are crying;
        Love's darts in May are flying.
So in the woods we sing and shout,
    Heigh-tralala loud ringing;
We sing, while all things bud and sprout,
    To May our welcome bringing."

Long the plaudits, loud the clapping,
When it ended. And the ladies
Also seemed delighted with it;
As, indeed, in the loud chorus
Many gentle female voices
Readily could be distinguished.
Margaret in playful humour,

Out of hazel-leaves and holly,
And of violets and crowfoot,
Wound a garland, and said archly:
"This wreath to the most deserving!
But I'm puzzled who shall get it—
Whether he who sang the May-song,
Or else he who on the trumpet
Played the fine accompaniment."

Said the Baron: "In this matter
I will give a just decision.
Ever the first prize is given
To the poet; but a garland
Or a laurel-crown, what are they?
I agree with the old Grecians
Who awarded to the singer
Just the victim's fattest portion,
As the saddle or the buttock.
And I fancy that the teacher's
Stores are not so well provided,
That he'll offer an objection.
Therefore I make him a present
Of the largest pike and carp, which
Still are left among our booty.
But as my young friend, the trumpeter,
Seems disposed less practically,
So you may, in my opinion,
Honour him with your fair garland:
For, indeed, he played not badly."

Simpering now the happy singer
Rubbed his hands and blessed the May-time,
As he saw a glowing vision
Of the pan with fishes frying.
But young Werner to the maiden
Bashfully approached, and lowly
Bending on his knee, he hardly
Dared to gaze at her blue eyes.
But with grace placed Margaretta
On his brow the blooming garland,
While a weird and lurid fire-light
Suddenly in fitful flashes
Fell upon the group assembled.
For the embers on the hearth-stone
Had ignited the old pine-tree.
Flaming fiery tongues now glided
Through the branches full of resin;
And the sparks flew crackling upward
Wildly to the evening sky.

Margaretta, Margaretta!
Were they fireworks which the pine woods
Fondly burned to do thee honour?
Or did Cupid with his flaming
Love-torch wander through the forest?
But the flames were soon extinguished,
And the Baron now gave orders
That the party should break up; and
Fishers, riders, noble ladies,

All went homeward in the twilight.
Faintly glimmering fell the last bright
Sparks from out the pine-tree branches,
Sinking in the mountain-lake.

EIGHTH PART.

THE CONCERT IN THE GARDEN PAVILION.

In the garden of the castle
Mighty chestnut trees are standing,
And a pretty gay pavilion.
In the Rhine are deeply sunken
The foundations of the terrace.
'Tis a quiet cosy corner,
Hidden by a mass of foliage,
While below the waves are murmuring.

For the last two months, mysterious
Business has been going on here.
Pots of colours, painting brushes,
Lime and mortar, masons' trowels
And high scaffoldings are rising
To the dome of the pavilion.
Is't some evil spirit's workshop?—
'Tis no evil spirit's workshop.
Frescoes here are being painted,

And the legs which there are dangling
From the lofty wooden scaffold,
Are the legs of the illustrious
Fresco-painter Fludribus,
Who returning from Italia
Had been living in the Rhine-land.
He was pleased with the fair country,
And the rosy happy faces,
And the cellars full of wine.
All the people wondered at him
As they would at an enchanter;
For he told them marvellous stories.
In his youth he had been travelling,
And by chance once in Bologna
Came upon the school of artists.
In the studio of Albini
He became a colour-mixer;
And from this most graceful master
He found out with ready cunning
How to paint both gods and heroes,
And the airy little cupids.
Yes, he even helped the master,
Making easy light gradations,
Or preparing the dead colouring.

On the Rhine, far round the country
Fludribus was the sole artist,
Painted many tavern sign-boards,
Pictures also for the chapels,

Portraits e'en of brides of peasants.
Stable was his reputation;
For if any criticisers
Would find fault with his great paintings,
That an arm or nose was crooked,
Or a cheek looked too much swollen,
Then he would o'erwhelm his critics
With the big high-sounding phrases
He had learnt when at Bologna.
Hearing nothing but perspective,
Colouring and soft gradation,
Modelling and bold foreshortening,
Soon they lost their wits entirely.

 Margaretta, who with faithful
Love had long the matter pondered,
How she would surprise her father
With a pleasure on his birthday,
Spoke to Master Fludribus:
"I have heard it oft related
How in France in lordly castles
They adorn the walls with frescoes.
Therefore try to paint now something
Like them here in my pavilion.
From the world secluded, I know
Naught about such compositions;
Therefore to your taste I leave all,
Only you must work in secret,
As the Baron must know nothing."

Fludribus looked consequential:
"Though but trifling is the order,
Still I coincide with Cæsar,
And am rather here considered
First than at great Rome the second.
And besides, there all is finished.
Even in the Pope's own palace
All those thoughts high and æsthetic,
Which I in my bosom cherished,
Has a man by name of Raphael
Painted on the walls already.
But I shall great things achieve,
And shall do like Buffamalco,
Who with rich red wine imparted
Glowing warmth to the cold colours.
Therefore, furnish me with red wine
First; of course, good eating with it.
Rich reward I do not care for,
Since the thought is my enjoyment,
That I shall be made immortal
Through the efforts of my genius.
Thus I'll paint for almost nothing,
Just the square foot seven shillings.

Since two months he had been painting
On the walls beneath the arched roof;
Imitated Buffamalco;
But he drank himself the red wine.
And his compositions truly

Were artistic, highly proper,
And of elegant conception.

To begin with : there paraded
Perseus and Andromeda ;
At their feet lay deadly wounded
The great Hydra, with a handsome
Face, much like a human being,
Who in dying still coquetted
With the lovely rock-bound captive.
Then the Judgment came of Paris ;
And in order that the dazzling
Beauty of those heavenly ladies
Should not quite eclipse the hero,
They looked off toward the landscape,
With their backs to the spectator.
Similar were the other pictures :
As Diana and Actæon,
Orpheus and Eurydice.
For the man of genius chooses
From mythology his subjects ;
And he thinks, in nudeness only,
Is revealed the highest beauty.
Now the work was all accomplished,
And with feeling, said the master :
" Happy can I go to Hades,
As my works are my memorial.
In the history of this Rhine-land

A new epoch of the fine arts
Will begin with Fludribus."

'Twas the wish of Margaretta
To inaugurate with music
This so beautified pavilion.
Ha! how Werner's heart was beating,
When he heard the maid's desire.
He directly went to Basel
To select the new productions
Of the musical composers;
And he brought the scores back with him
Of the great Venetian master,
Claudio di Monteverde,
Whose sweet pastoral composition
Carried off the prize in music.
Then there was a noisy bustle
'Mongst the artists of the city;
And a most increasing practice
In the frequent long rehearsals,
All unnoticed by the Baron.

Now, at last, the long-expected
Day had come, the Baron's birthday.
At the table he was chatting
With his friend and pleasant neighbour,
The good prelate of St. Blasien,
Who had driven hither early,
To express his heartfelt wishes.

Meanwhile many hands were busy
Decorating the pavilion
With fresh garlands, and were placing
Rows of music-desks in order.

By degrees there came now gliding
Through the side-gate by the river
All the musical performers.
First, the youthful burgomaster
Bending under the unwieldy
Contra-bass, whose sounds sonorous
Often from his thoughts did banish
All the cares of his high office,
And the council's stupid blunders.
Next there came the bloated chaplain
Who played finely on the violin,
Drawing from it such shrill wailings,
As if wishing to give utterance
To his lonely bachelor's heart.
With his horn beneath his arm came
The receiver's clerk, who often,
A great bore to his superior,
With his playing did enliven
All the dry accounts he summed up,
And the dulness of subtraction.
There came also stepping slowly,
Dressed in black, but shabby looking,
With a hat the worse for usage,
He the lank assistant-teacher,

EIGHTH PART.

Who by Art consoled himself for
What was wanting in his income,
And instead of wine and roast beef
Lived upon his flute's sweet music.
Then came——Who can count, however,
All these instrumental players?
All the talent of the city
For this concert had united.
From the ironworks of Albbruck
Even came the superintendent;
He alone played the viola.

Like a troop of mounted warriors
Who the enemy expecting,
Lurk in safe and hidden ambush,
So they waited for the Baron
To arrive. And like good marksmen
Who with care before the battle
Try their weapons, if their powder
By the dew has not been damaged,
If the flint is good for striking;
So by blowing, scraping, tuning,
They their instruments were trying.

Margaretta led the Baron
And his guest now to the garden.
Women never are in want of
A good pretext, when some fun or
Some surprise they are preparing.

So she praised the shady coolness
And the view from the pavilion,
Till the two old friends were turning
Toward that spot without suspicion.
Like a volley then resounded
At their entrance a loud flourish,
Every instrument saluting;
And like roaring torrents bursting
Wildly through the gaping sluice-gate,
So the overture let loose now
Its loud storming floods of music
On the much astonished hearers.
With the greatest skill young Werner
Led the orchestra, whose chorus
Gladly yielded to his bâton.
Ha! that was a splendid bowing,
Such a fiddling, such a pealing!
Hopping lightly, like a locust,
Through the din the clarinet flew,
And the contra-bass kept groaning,
As if wailing for its soul,
While the player's brow was sweating
From his arduous performance.

There behind in the orchestra
Fludribus the drum was beating;
As a many-sided genius,
During pauses, he was also
To the triangle attending.

EIGHTH PART.

But his heart o'erflowed with sadness;
And the drum's dull sound re-echoed
His complaints, as dull and grumbling:
"Dilettanti, happy people!
Merrily they suck the honey
From the flowers which with heavy
Throes the Master's mind created;
And they spice well their enjoyment
With their mutual frequent blunders.
Genuine Art is a titanic
Heaven-storming strife and struggle
For a Beauty still receding,
While the soul is gnawed with longing
For the unattained Ideal.
But these bunglers are quite happy."

Now the din of sound subsided.
As oft after heavy tempests,
When the thunder ceases pealing,
Mildly shineth forth the rainbow
'Gainst the canopy of heaven;
So now the full band is followed
By the trumpet's dulcet solo.
Werner blew it: low and melting
Rang the tunes forth from the trumpet.
Full of wonder some were staring
At the score, in wonder also
The fat chaplain nudged the teacher
On the arm, and whispered softly:

"Hear'st thou what he's playing? Nothing
Like it in the score is written.
Has he read perhaps his music
In the fair young lady's eyes?"

Splendidly the concert came thus
To an end, and the musicians
Sat exhausted and yet happy
That they had so well succeeded.
Now the prelate of St. Blasien
Stepped forth bowing quite politely
To the band, and as a clever
Connoisseur and statesman spoke thus:
"Heavy wounds have been inflicted
On our land while war was raging,
And throughout our German country
Rudeness was predominating.
Therefore it deserves great praise, thus
With the Muses to take refuge.
This refreshes and ennobles,
Civilises human beings,
So that war and strife are silenced.
All these frescoes on the walls here
Show no ordinary talent;
And still more this feast of music
Makes me think well of the players
Who my ears have thus delighted,
Brought my happy youth before me,
Took me back to fair Italia,

When in Rome I listened to the
Tones of Cavalieri's Daphne,
And idyllic pastoral longing
Filled my heart to overflowing.
Therefore, my dear friends, continue
Thus to worship at Art's altar.
Let the harmony of sound keep
Far from you all strife and discord.
Oh how pleasant it would be, if
Such a spirit were but common!"

Deeply moved by these high praises
From a man of such rich knowledge,
The whole orchestra, delighted,
Bowed to him when he had finished.
Highly pleased, the Baron also
Walked around, gave hearty greetings;
And to testify his thanks—for
Words alone don't suit a Baron—
Ordered from his well-stocked cellars
A huge cask of beer brought up there.
'Twas well done, my good musicians,
Most efficient chapel-master!
Where the devil have you picked up
All these pretty compositions?
And you, Fludribus, have also
Painted well; suits me exactly.
Other times, 'tis true, may come yet
When our goddesses must wear more

Draperies than you have painted;
But a gray old soldier does not
Blame you for a little nudeness.
Therefore, let us ring our glasses
To our noble guest's good health, and
To the excellent musicians.
Yes, for aught I care, we'll drink to
The fair shivering painted deities,
That the winter in the Rhine-land
May not prove too rigorous for them."

Margaretta thought it wiser
Now to leave the room, well knowing
That the party might get noisy.
On the threshold she gave Werner
Her fair hand with grateful feeling.
'Tis most likely that the pressure
Of the hand was full of meaning;
But no chronicle doth tell us:
Was it homage to the artist,
Or a sign of deeper interest?

Glasses rang and foaming bumpers,
And there was some heavy drinking;
But my song must keep the secret
Of the fate of late returners;
Also hide the sudden drowning
Which the hat of the lank teacher
Suffered in the Rhine that night.

But at midnight, when the last guest
For his home long since had started,
Low the chestnut trees were whispering.
Said the one: " Oh fresco paintings ! "
Said the other : " Oh thou ding dong ! "
Then the first : " I see the future—
See there two remorseless workmen,
See two monstrous painting-brushes,
See two buckets full of whitewash.
And they quietly daub over,
With a heavy coating, heroes,
Deities, and Fludribus.
Other ages—other pictures ! "

Said the other : " In the far-off
Future I hear from the same place
Glees resounding from male voices,
Rising to our lofty summits,
Simple touching German music.
Other ages—other music ! "
Both together added : " True love
Will endure throughout all ages ! "

NINTH PART.

TEACHING AND LEARNING.

WINDS and the swift river's current
Hardly had swept off the dulcet
Melodies of Monteverde,
When the people in the city
Held no other conversation
Than of this great feast of music.
Not, however, of the spirit
Of the melodies they'd heard then,
Neither of the deep emotion
Which was in their souls awakened,
Were they speaking; they disputed
Who received the Baron's thanks first
At the end of the performance;
Whom the Abbot had distinguished
Most that evening by his praises;
And what finally was served up
From the kitchen and the cellar.
As the tail of a dead lizard

Still, when life has long departed,
With spasmodic jerks is writhing :
So the memory of great actions
Still lives on in daily gossip.
But with thoughts above such nonsense
Margaretta took an early
Solitary walk next morning
To the honeysuckle arbour,
There to dream of last night's music,
Specially of Werner's solo,
Which still through her soul was thrilling
Like a message of sweet love.
But what saw she ?   In the arbour
On the little rustic table
She beheld the very trumpet.
Like the magic horn of Huon,
Wondrous mysteries containing ;
Dumb, but full of deep expression,
Like a star it sparkled there.

Margaretta stood confounded
At the arbour's shady entrance :
" Came he here ?   And now, where is he ?
Wherefore has he left his trumpet
Here so wholly unprotected ?
Easily a worm might crawl in,
Or a thief might come and steal it.
Shall I take it to the castle,
Take it in my careful keeping ?

No, I'll go, do nothing with it,
Should indeed have gone before."

But she tarried, for her eyes were
Held in durance by the trumpet,
Like a shad caught by the fish-hook.
"Oh, I wonder," she was thinking,
"Whether my breath would be able
From its depths a tone to waken.
Oh I much should like to know this!
No one sees what I am doing,
All around no living being.
Only my old Hiddigeigei
Licks the dew from off the box-tree;
Only insects in the sand here
Follow out their digging instinct,
And the caterpillars gently
Up and down the arbour crawl."

So the maiden shyly entered,
Shyly she took up the trumpet,
To her rosy lips she pressed it;
But with fright she well-nigh trembled
At her breath to sound transforming
In the trumpet's golden calyx,
Which the air was bearing farther,
Farther—ah, who knoweth where?
But she cannot stop the fun now,
And with sounds discordant, horrid,

Fit to rend the ears to pieces,
So disturbed the morning stillness,
That the poor cat Hiddigeigei's
Long black hair stood up like bristles,
Like the sharp quills of a hedgehog.
Raising then his paw to cover
His offended ear, he spoke thus :
" Suffer on, my valiant cat-heart,
Which so much has borne already,
Also bear this maiden's music !
We, we understand the laws well,
Which do regulate and govern
Sound, enigma of creation.
And we know the charm mysterious
Which invisibly through space floats,
And, intangible a phantom,
Penetrates our hearing organs,
And in beasts' as well as men's hearts
Wakes up love, delight and longing,
Raving madness and wild frenzy.
And yet, we must bear this insult,
That when nightly in sweet mewing
We our love-pangs are outpouring,
Men will only laugh and mock us,
And our finest compositions
Rudely brand as caterwauling.
And in spite of this we witness
That these same fault-finding beings
Can produce such horrid sounds as

Those which I have just now heard.
Are such tones not like a nosegay
Made of straw, and thorns, and nettles,
In the midst a prickly thistle?
And in presence of this maiden
Who the trumpet there is blowing,
Can a man then without blushing
E'er sneer at our caterwauling?
But, thou valiant heart, be patient!
Suffer now, the time will yet come
When this self-sufficient monster,
Man, will steal from us the true art
Of expressing all his feelings;
When the whole world in its struggle
For the highest form of culture
Will adopt our style of music.
For in history, there is justice,
She redresses every wrong."

But besides old Hiddigeigei,
Standing far down by the river
There was still another listener
To these first attempts at blowing,
Who felt anger more than pleasure.

It was Werner. He came early
With his trumpet to the garden,
Wanted to compose a song there
In that quiet morning-hour.

First, however, his dear trumpet
He laid on the rustic table,
Then stood musing by the stone-wall
Gazing at the rapid river.
"Yes, I see, your waves preserve still
Their old course and disposition,
Ever toward the ocean rushing,
As my heart for my love striveth.
Who now from the goal is farthest,
Clear green river, thou or I?"
All this train of thought was broken
By the stork from the old tower,
Who, full of a father's pride, had
Taken his young brood to ramble
On the Rhine-shore for the first time.
'Twas amusing to young Werner
How just then the old stork gravely,
On the sand with stealthy cunning,
Closely a poor eel was watching,
Who of various worms was making
There a comfortable meal.
He, however, who was wielding
O'er the little worms the strand-law,
Soon himself will serve as breakfast.
For the greater eats the lesser,
And the greatest eats the great ones.
In this simple manner nature
Solves the knotty social question.
No more did his smoothness help him,

No more his sleek body's wriggling,
No more his spasmodic beating
With his tail so strong and supple.
Tightly held in the indented
Beak of the determined parent,
He was given to the hopeful
Stork-brood, now to be divided;
And they held with noisy clatter
Solemnly their morning-feast.
Nearer to observe this, Werner
Had descended to the Rhine-bank,
And he seemed in no great hurry
To commence his composition.
There he sat himself down gently
On the insect-covered moss-bank,
Shaded by a silvery willow,
And it gave him much amusement
Thus to be a silent witness
Of this banquet of the storks.

Pleasures, yet, of all descriptions
Are but fleeting on our planet.
Even to the most contented
Doth it happen that fate often
Like a meteor bursts upon them.
Only a short time had Werner
Viewed this scene when he was startled
By the tones of his own trumpet,

Which like keen-edged Pandour daggers
Deep into his soul were cutting.

"'Tis the gardener's saucy youngster
Who my trumpet thus is blowing,"
Said young Werner, in his anger
Starting from his seat so quickly
That the storks thereby much frightened,
Fluttering upward sought the tower;
And so quickly that they even
Had no time to take the eel off.
Like a poor old torso lay he
On the sand so pitifully;
And the chronicles are silent
Whether the old father stork came
Ever back to take his booty.

Werner meanwhile to the garden
Climbed up; to the shady arbour
On the soft green sward he's walking,
That the pebbly footpath may not
By the noise betray his coming.
In the very act of sinning
Doth he wish to catch the rascal,
And to beat time to his music
On his back without relenting.
Thus he comes up to the arbour,
With his hand raised high in anger.
But, as if 'twere struck by lightning,

To his side it dropped down quickly,
And the stroke remained, like German
Unity and other projects,
Only an ideal dream.
Then beheld he Margaretta
Pressing to her lips the trumpet,
And her rosy cheeks are puffed out
Like those trumpet-blowing angels'
In the church of Fridolinus.
Up she starts now as a thief would
In the neighbour's yard detected,
And the trumpet drops abruptly
From the touch of her soft lips.
Werner covered her confusion
Through a clever maze of language;
And with ardour he commences
On the spot to teach the maiden
The first steps in trumpet-blowing
In strict order, with due method;
Shows the instrument's construction,
How to use the lips in blowing,
That true tones may be forthcoming.
Margaretta listened docile,
And before she is aware, new
Tones she finds she is awaking
From the trumpet which young Werner
With low bows had handed to her.
Easily from him she learneth
What her father's cuirassiers blew

As the call to charge in battle ;
Only a few notes and simple,
But most pithy and inspiring.

  Love is, there can be no question,
Of all teachers the most skilful ;
And what years of earnest study
Do not conquer, he is winning
With the charm of an entreaty,
With the magic of a look.
E'en a common Flemish blacksmith
Once became through love's sweet passion
In advanced age a great painter.
Happy teacher, happy scholar,
In the honeysuckle arbour !
'Twas as if the only safety
Of the German empire rested
On this trumpet-call's performance.
But within their souls was stirring
Quite a different melody :
That sweet song, old as creation,
Of the bliss of youthful lovers ;
True, a song without the words yet,
But they had divined its meaning,
And beneath a playful manner
Hid the blissful consciousness.
Startled by this trumpet-blowing
Came the Baron reconnoitring,
Tried to frown, but soon his anger

Was converted into pleasure,
When he heard his child there blowing
The old fanfar of his horsemen.
Friendly spoke he to young Werner:
"You are truly in your office
A most ardent zeal unfolding.
If you go on in this manner,
We shall see most wondrous things yet.
The old stable-door which harshly
Creaks and groans upon its hinges,
Even in the pond the bull-frogs
May perhaps change for the better,
Through your trumpet's magic charm."

Werner held, however, henceforth
His dear trumpet as a jewel,
Which the richest Basel merchant,
With the fullest bag of money,
Could not ever purchase from him;
For the lips of Margaretta
Made it sacred by their touch.

TENTH PART.

YOUNG WERNER IN THE GNOME'S CAVE.

From the Feldberg tears a raging
Foaming torrent through the forests
To the Rhine—its name is Wehra.
In the narrow valley standeth
'Midst the rocks a single fir-tree;
In the branches sat the haggard
Wicked wood-sprite Meysenhartus,
Who to-day behaved quite badly:
Showing his sharp teeth and grinning,
Tore a branch off from the fir-tree,
And kept gnawing at a pine-cone;
Clambered often quite indignant
Up and down just like a squirrel;
From the wings of a poor night-owl
Roughly plucked out several feathers;
And while mocking the old fir-tree
Rocked himself upon its summit.

"High old fir-tree, green old fir-tree!
I with thee would ne'er my lot change.
Firmly rooted must thou stand there,
And take everything that happens;
Never canst thou quit thy station.
And if ever Fate ordaineth,
Thou to far-off lands shalt wander,
Men have first to come with axes;
With hard strokes they hack and cut thee,
Deep into thy flesh, till falling;
And then strip unmercifully
All thy skin from off thy body;
Throw thee next into the Rhine, and
Make thee swim as far as Holland.
And if e'er they pay the honour
On a frigate to erect thee
As a proud and stately mast, still
Thou art but a smooth-skinned fir-tree,
Without roots there lonely standing;
And thou yearnest on the ocean
For thy old home in the forest,
Till at last a flash of lightning
Mast and ship and all destroyeth.
High old fir-tree, green old fir-tree!
I with thee would ne'er my lot change!"

Said the fir-tree: "Everybody
Must accept the sphere he's born in,
And fulfil his duties fully.

So we think here in the forest;
And 'tis well so, at least better
Than to hop will-o'-the-wisp like,
Playing pranks and doing mischief,
Men and cattle oft misleading,
And the stupid wanderer's curses
As reward home with thee taking.
Anyhow, no one cares for thee.
For, at best, a peasant sayeth,
Devil take this Meysenhartus!
But they're others who write volumes
Proving thou hast no existence;
That to lose one's way at night-time
Comes from fogs and drunken frolics.
Oh the spirit-shares stand badly!
On the highway I would rather
As a paving-stone be lying,
Than to be a third-class spirit,
Like the wood-sprite Meysenhartus."

Said the spirit: "Thou knowest nothing
Of all this, my noble fir-tree.
Meysenhartus and his brothers
O'er the globe rule powerfully;
Everywhere throughout creation
Are wrong tracks, and also people
Who upon these same paths wander.
And whenever, gay or mournful,
Someone goes upon a wrong track,

He has been by us deluded.
Let them doubt if there are spirits;
Still they are in our dominion.
And to-day you'll see me leading
Someone far astray to show him
That the spirits are in numbers."

From the hill came Master Werner.
Deeply musing o'er his love-dream
He had wandered through the forest,
And as far as man is happy
Here below, he was; and buoyant
Hope and joy his heart were filling.
Many burning thoughts were passing
Through his brain, as if they shortly
Into love-songs might be growing,
Just as caterpillars later
Into butterflies develop.
Homeward now he would be turning;
But the wood-sprite Meysenhartus
Hid with dust the right path from him,
And young Werner, absent-minded,
'Stead of river-ward went inland.
Now again the wood-sprite grinning
Clambered to the fir-tree's summit,
Rocking gaily in the branches.
"He is caught!" so said he, mocking.
Werner paying no attention,
Went up through the Hasel valley,
Till he came to a steep mountain,

To a corner cool and shady.
Holly, sloe, and climbing ivy
Grew around the rocks luxuriant,
While near by a clear spring rippled.

Through the bushes stepped young Werner
To refresh himself by drinking.
Strongly tangled was the brushwood,
And upon it he trod firmly.
Then upon his ear broke squeaking
Wailing tones, as from a mole which
At his subterranean labour
Caught in traps and now detected,
Roughly is jerked up to daylight.
From the grass rose something crackling;
Lo, there stood a gray-clad pygmy,
Hardly three feet high, and hunchbacked;
But his face was clear and gentle,
And his odd small eyes looked clever.
Gracefully he let the long ends
Of his garment on the ground trail,
And said, limping: "Sir, you have been
Treading on my foot most rudely."
Said young Werner: "I am sorry."
Now the pygmy: "And what business
Have you in our vale at all?"
Said young Werner: "I by no means
Wish to seek for the acquaintance
Of such injudicious pygmies,

Who like grasshoppers are skipping,
And are asking silly questions."
Said the pygmy: " Thus ye all speak,
All ye rude and clumsy mortals;
Ever with your big feet tramping
Till the ground beneath you trembles.
And yet you are only clinging
To the surface like the chafers
Which are nestling in the tree-bark;
Thinking that you rule creation,
But entirely ignoring
All those spirits which, though silent,
On the heights, in depths, are working.
Oh ye rude and clumsy mortals!
Shut up proudly in your houses,
You are groaning with hard labour.
In the hot-house of your noddles
Are some plants called art and science,
And you even brag of such weeds.
By the lime-spar and rock-crystal!
You have much to learn, I tell you,
Ere the truth you will see dawning!"

Said young Werner: " It is lucky
That to-day I feel so peaceful,
Else I should have taken pleasure
By your long gray beard to hang you
On the holly bushes yonder!
But my heart to-day is glowing

With the sunshine of my love-dreams,
Which you with your spars and crystals
Never can be comprehending.
Oh, to-day I could embrace all,
And be kind to everybody.
Say then who you are, and whether
I can be of any service."

Then the dwarf said: "This sounds better.
To your questions I will answer.
To the race of gnomes belong I,
Who in crevices are living;
Down in subterranean caverns,
Watch there gold and silver treasures,
Grind and polish bright the crystals,
Carry coals to the eternal
Fire in the earth's deep centre;
And we heat there well. Without us
You here would have long since frozen.
From Vesuvius and Mount Etna
You can see our furnace smoking.
E'en for you ungrateful mortals,
Though unseen, we're ever working;
And sweet lullabies are singing
In the mountains to your rivers,
That no harm they may be doing;
Keep the crumbling rocks from falling,
Chain the ice up in the glaciers;
Boil for you the pungent rock-salt,

Also mix much healing matter
With the springs from which you're drinking.
Never ceasing, and enormous
Is the gray gnomes' daily labour
In the bowels of the earth.
Formerly they used to know us;
Wise and clever men and women,
Grave old priests descended to us
In the depths, where to our labour
They oft listened, and they spoke thus:
" In the caves the gods are dwelling."
But you have become estranged since;
Still, we willingly will open
To your gaze our hidden treasures;
And we hold in great affection
All the travelling German scholars;
For their hearts are kind and generous,
And they see much more than others.
You seem also one, so follow!
Here my cave is, in this valley:
If you can but stoop a little,
I will show you where to enter."

Said young Werner: "I am ready."
Thereupon the little pygmy
From the rock pushed back some brushwood.
When appeared a small low passage.
"Light is needed here for mortals,"
Said the gnome, who now was rubbing

Two hard flints, and soon had lighted
By the sparks a piece of pine-wood.
With this torch he went ahead then;
Werner followed, often stooping,
Often even well-nigh creeping,
For the rocks were nearly meeting.
Soon, however, widely opened
At the passage end a cavern
Of gigantic height and grandeur.
Slender columns there supported
Lofty arches of the ceiling;
From the walls the gray stalactites
Hung in various patterns twining,
Marvellous, yet graceful textures;
Some like tears which from the walls dropped,
Others like the richly twisted
Branches of gigantic corals.
An unearthly bluish colour
All throughout the space was glowing,
Mingled with the glaring torch-light
From the sharp-edged stones reflected.
From the depths a rushing sound rose
As from distant mountain-streams.
Werner gazed at all this splendour,
Felt as in a dream transported
To some strange and lofty temple,
And his heart was filled with awe.

"My young friend," now said the pygmy,

"Tell me, pray, what are you thinking
Of the gnome's secluded dwelling?
This is but a place for work-days.
Fairer ones far in the North lie,
Also in the Alpine caverns;
But Italia owns the fairest,
On the rocky shore of Capri,
In the Mediterranean Sea.
O'er the sea's blue waters rise up
The stalactites' lofty arches,
And the waves in the dark cavern
With blue magic light are gleaming,
And the tide protects the entrance.
The Italian gnomes there often
Bathe and frolic with the daughters
Of old Nereus, the sea-god,
And the sailor shuns the grotto.
But perhaps in later ages
May a sunday-child look in there,
Like thyself a travelling minstrel,
Or a merry-hearted artist.
But now, come, we must go farther!"

Downward stepped he with the torch-light
Ever farther. Werner saw how
Huge chaotic rocky masses
Lay in heaps of wild confusion,
Over which was rushing foaming,
To the bottomless abyss, a river.

Over steep and high rocks clambering,
They now entered a new passage.
It looked home-like, a large square-room,
Of high rocky walls constructed,
Fitted for a hermitage;
Round about stood slender columns.
Ever dropping from the ceiling
And through centuries increasing
Had stalactites slowly formed them;
And some others stood half finished
In the process of formation.
Now the gnome knocked on the columns,
And mysterious solemn tones rang
Out in deep harmonious rhythm.
"They are tuned," he said, "according
To the harmony of the spheres."

In this room a rock was lying.
Smooth and round, just like a table;
And there motionless and silent
Sat a man—looked as if sleeping,
Leaned his head upon his right hand.
Stony were his lordly features,
And the flame of life no longer
Played o'er them; and doubtless many
Tears had his sad eyes been shedding.
Petrified they now were hanging
In his beard and from his robes.
Werner gazed at him with terror

And he asked: "Is this a statue,
Or a man of flesh and blood?"

Said the gnome: "This is my guest here.
'Tis the *silent man*, whom many
Years I've comfortably sheltered.
Once he was a proud old mortal,
And I found him in the valley,
And I offered then to show him
Where to find the nearest village.
But he shook his head and broke out
In a mocking scornful laughter.
Marvellously grand his words were,
Now like prayers devout and pious,
Like a psalm, such as we gnomes sing
Often in the earth's vast bowels;
Then like curses unto heaven.
Much I could not understand,
But it woke the recollections
Of the days of time primeval,
When the wild ferocious Titans
Rocks and mountains tore up o'er us
From their firm and deep foundations,
And we fled to greater depths.
For the man I felt great pity,
And I took him to my cavern;
And he liked it, when I showed him
All the gnomes' incessant labours;
And directly felt at home here.

Oft together have we listened
To the growing of stalactites,
Chatted also many evenings
Of the things below us hidden;
Only when my conversation
Turned to men, he grew quite angry;
Dark his frowns were, and he broke once
Seven columns in his fury.
When I wished to praise the sunlight
And the skies, he stopped me, saying:
'Speak not of the sky or sunlight!
In the sunlight there above us
Snakes are creeping, and they sting one;
Men are living and they hate one;
Up there in the starry heavens
We see questions which are waiting
For an answer; who can give it?'
So he stayed here in the cavern,
And the grief which overwhelmed him
Was dissolved in tender sadness.
Oft I saw him gently weeping;
Oft, when a melodious wailing
Through the columns' hollow shafts rang,
He sat there, his sweet songs singing.
But he gradually grew silent.
Did I ask him what he wanted,
Then he smiling took my hand:
'Gnome, I many songs can sing thee,
But the best I have not sung yet.

Will you know its name? 'Tis silence.
Silence—silence! oh how well one
Learns it here in thy deep cavern;
Depth creates true modesty.
But the cold is o'er me creeping;
Gnome! 'tis true, my poor heart freezes.
Gnome! dost thou know what true love is?
If for diamonds thou art digging,
And dost find them, take them with thee,
Guard them safely in thy cavern.
Gnome, thy heart will never freeze then!'

"These the last words he has spoken.
Now for years he has been silent
In this spot. He has not died yet
Nor is living, but his body
Slowly into stone is changing;
And I nurse him; heartfelt pity
For my silent guest I cherish,
Often try to cheer his spirit
With the columns' solemn music,
And I know it pleases him.
Without taking any freedom,
I think you too are a minstrel;
And the service you can do me
Is to play before my guest here."

Then young Werner took his trumpet
And began to play; his mournful

Strains were ringing through the cavern
As if breathing forth deep pity.
Then in thinking of his own love,
Through the sadness now there mingled
Strains of joy—first faint and distant,
Then came nearer—fresher, fuller,
And the last notes sounded like a
Glorious hymn on Easter morning.
And the silent man then listened,
Nodded gently with his head.
Fare-thee-well, dream on in peace, thou
Silent man, in thy still cavern,
Till the fulness comes of knowledge
And of love, to wake the sleeper.

Through the winding cave young Werner
With the gnome was now returning.
As the spacious dome they entered
A great rock the gnome uplifted.
Underneath a shrine was hidden,
And within were sparkling jewels.
Also writings and old parchments.
One pale amethyst, and papers
Which by age had turned quite yellow,
Gave the gnome now to young Werner,
Saying: "Take these as mementoes!
If the world above doth vex thee,
Here thou e'er wilt find a refuge.
But when wicked men are saying

That gnomes' feet are webbed like geese-feet,
Then, by lime-spar and rock-crystal!
Say that they are dreadful liars.
True, our soles are somewhat flattened;
But 'tis only a rude peasant
Who so cruelly maligns us.
Now good-bye, there is the outlet;
Take the pine-torch, light thyself now,
I have other things to do."—
Spoke and crept into a crevice.

Musing through the narrow passage
Went young Werner, and his head struck
Oft against the rocky ceiling
Ere he reached again the daylight.
Peacefully the evening-bell rang
Through the vale as he went homeward.

ELEVENTH PART.

THE HAUENSTEIN RIOT.

Through the Schwarzwald spreads a buzzing,
Buzzing as of bees when swarming,
As of the approaching storm-wind.
In the tavern savage fellows
Meet: their heavy fists are striking
On the table: " Bring me wine here !
Better times are now approaching
For this land of Hauenstein."
From the corn-loft brings the peasant
His old-fashioned rusty musket,
Which below the floor was hidden;
Fetches also the long halberd.
On the walnut-tree the raven
Harshly croaks : " Long have I fasted :
Soon I'll have meat for my dinner,
I shall relish thee, poor peasant !"

Now the people from the mountains
Throng at Herrischried the market;

There the seat is of their union,
There they hold their union-meeting.
But to-day the Hauenstein peasants
Came not in black velvet doublets,
With red stomachers and white frills,
As was usually their custom.
Some had buckled on cuirasses,
Others wore their leather doublets;
In the breeze the flag was waving,
And the morning sun was shining
On their spears and thick spiked clubs.
Near the old church in the market
Stood the village elders, with the
Union-leader and mace-bearer.
"Silence, men!" the beadle shouted.
Silence reigned, and on the church-steps
Mounted then the peasants' speaker,
Holding an official paper,
Stroked his long gray beard, and said:

"Inasmuch as the hard war-time
Has much injured town and country,
And the debt is much augmented;
So to meet increased expenses
Our most gracious rulers hereby
Do exact new contributions;
Seven florins from each household,
And from all the bachelors two.
And next week the tax-collector

ELEVENTH PART.   171

Comes to gather these new taxes.
So 'tis written in this paper."
—" Death upon the tax-collector !
May God damn him ! " cried the people.—
" Now as we ourselves have suffered
Quite enough by this sad war, and
Many lost their goods and chattels ;
And because 'tis pledged in writing
As one of our privileges,
That there shall be no new taxes
E'er imposed upon this country,
Many this demand consider
As a most unjust extortion,
Think we should stand up most firmly
For our ancient rights by charter,
And should never pay a farthing."
—" Not a farthing ! " cried the people.—
" So we summoned you together
For your final resolution."

   Like the distant surf their voices
Loudly roared in wild confusion :
" Come ! stand up ! speak out ! We must now
Hear the Bergalingen Fridli.
He knows best—and all we others
Always are of his opinion."
Then stepped out the man thus called for,
And upon a big log mounting,
Spoke thus with a shrewd expression :

"Do you see at last, dull peasants,
What the end will be? Your fathers
Once gave up their little finger;
Now they want to seize the whole hand.
Only give it, and you'll soon see,
How they'll flay your very skin off!
Who can really thus compel us?
In his woods free lives the peasant,
Nothing but the sun above him.
So it stands in our old records,
In the statutes of our union:
Nothing there of rent and socage,
Nothing of a bondman's service!
But there's danger we shall have them.
Do you know what will protect us?
Yonder there the Swiss can tell you,
And the valiant Appenzellers.
This here!"—and he brandished fiercely
O'er his head his thick spiked club.—
"On the fir-tree I heard piping
Lately a white bird at midnight:
Good old time, that bygone time,
Peasants, freemen in their forests;
If with spears and guns you seek it,
You will see it soon returning.
Now, Amen! my speech is ended."

Then wild cries rose from the people.
"He is right" were many saying;

ELEVENTH PART.

"To the devil with our rulers!
Burn these damned taxation-papers!
All these scribblers may look out soon
If this flame can be extinguished
With the fluid in their inkstands."
Said another: "Thou, oh governor,
Didst consign me to a dungeon;
Poor my fare, with only water!
Thou hast wine within thy cellar,
And I hope we now shall try it.
Yes, with thee I'll square accounts soon!"
Said a third one: "Thee my musket,
Which has brought down many woodcocks,
I shall use for nobler sport soon.
Then hit well! For we'll be shooting
At the great black double eagle."
Thus a murmur through the crowd went.
Just as when the plague is raging,
Everywhere infection spreadeth,
So were all the peasants' hearts now
Filled with passion and blind wrath.
And in vain spoke the experienced
Villaringen elder, Balthes:

"If a horse's tail is bridled,
Not his mouth, no one can drive him.
If the peasant seeks for justice
By revolt, all will go badly;
In the end he gets a thrashing.

Hence of old we were commanded
To obey the ruling powers,
And——" but now involuntary
Was he stopped in his sage counsels:
"Turn him out, this old fool Balthes!
May God damn him! He is faithless;
He's a traitor to his country!"
Thus they howled out, stones were flying,
Spears were threatening, and his friends could
Hardly get him off in safety.

"To be short, what use of speaking?"
Fridli said, of Bergalingen.
"Who are faithful to our old rights
And will go for them to battle,
Raise their hands high!" And they raised them
All, while loud hurrahs they shouted.
Arms are clanking, flags are waving,
Battle-cries—the drums are beating.
And that day large bands were marching
From the hills toward the river
To attack the forest-cities.

In the forest from the fir-tree
Looked the wood-sprite Meysenhartus,
Mocking at the peasants' army,
Said: "A lucky journey to you!
No need I should now mislead you,
As you choose yourselves the wrong track!"

Scouts are riding, watchmen blowing,
Women wailing, children crying;
Through the vale rings the alarm-bell.
Burghers through the streets are running:
"Close the gates! Defend the town-walls!
Bring the guns up to the tower!"
From the terrace saw the Baron
This commotion in the forest,
How the mountain-paths were darkened
By the peasant-bands descending.
"Am I dreaming," said he, "or have
All these men indeed forgotten,
How a hundred and fifty years since
Such mad peasants' jokes were punished?
Yes, indeed, the forest glitters
With their helmets and their halberds.
Well devised, you cunning peasants!
While below there on the Danube
The proud eagle of the emperor
Lets the Turks feel his sharp talons,
You think that it will be easy,
On the Rhine to pluck his feathers!
Look out well that this your reckoning
Won't deceive you; and I swear here,
The old Baron will not fail to
Greet you with a warm reception."

Turned and went into the castle,
And he donned his leathern doublet,

Buckled on the heavy broadsword,
And gave orders to the household:
" Quickly get your weapons ready,
Keep good watch upon the towers,
Raise the drawbridge, and let no one,
While I am away, here enter!
Master Werner, you may order
All the rest. Protect my castle,
And my daughter, my chief treasure!
Have no fear, dear Margaretta;
Brave must be a soldier's child.
Only some few coal-black ravens
Come there flying from the forest,
Want to get their skulls well battered
'Gainst the walls of this good city.
God preserve you! I myself go
To my post, up to the town-hall."

Margaretta threw herself now
In the Baron's arms, who kindly
Pressed upon her brow fond kisses.
Shaking Werner's hand then warmly
He walked off unto the square.

There the ladies of the convent
Wailing went up to the minster:
" Show us mercy, Fridolinus!"
By his door the " Button " landlord
Asked the Baron: " Is it time now,

That we put our gold and silver
In the cellar's deepest places?"
Said the Baron: "Shame upon you!
It is time to take your weapons
And to help defend the city.
Show the same zeal as when fishing!"

In the town-hall were assembled
Councillors and burgomaster.
Many of the city-fathers
Made wry faces, as though fearing
The last judgment-day was coming.
On their hearts their sins were pressing
Like a hundredweight; they cried out:
"Save us, God, from this great evil,
And we'll promise all our lifetime
Ne'er to take unlawful interest,
Never to defraud the orphan,
Ne'er to mix sand with our spices."
Even one proposed this motion:
"Let us send out to these peasants
Meat and wine in great abundance,
Also of doubloons some dozens,
That from hence they may depart;
They in Waldshut may look out then,
How they drive away these fellows."

Now the Baron came among them:
"My good sirs! I do believe you

Hang your heads. To work now bravely!
When the Swedes the town beleagured,
Then 'twas grave, but this is only
Child's play. Surely you have always
Liked to hear and make good music;
So the booming guns will please you.
Let the orchestra strike up now!
And these fellows, when they hear you,
Homeward soon will all go dancing,
E'er the emperor's own detachment
Plays for them the grand finale."

 Thus he spoke. In times of terror
Oft a brave word at the right time
Can work wonders; many cowards
From example drink in courage;
And one single iron will leads
Oft along the wavering masses.
Thus the council looked up strengthened
To the Baron's gray moustaches.
" Yes, this is just our opinion,
We'll defend our city bravely,
And the Baron shall command us;
For he knows well how to do it.
Death to all these cursèd peasants!"
Through the streets th' alarm is sounded
To the town-gate, where a narrow
Dam leads on to terra firma,
Ran well armed the younger people.

On the bastion stood commanding
Fludribus, the fresco-painter,
Who had there assembled round him
Some young lads who with great effort
An old gun were hauling up there.
Smiling looked at them the Baron,
But great Fludribus said gravely:
"Devotees of art can boast of
Stores of universal knowledge.
Let them have a chance, and they will
Rule the state as well as armies.
My keen eye sees well there's danger
In this spot; and as Cellini
From the Castle of St. Angelo
Shot the constable of France once,
So—alas at foes inferior—
Cannonades here Fludribus."

"Only do not kill them all off!"
Said the Baron; "and be sure first
To get balls enough and powder;
For, the gun you there are dragging
Will not be of use without them!"

To the Rhine-bank came the peasants
In great crowds, and looked up growling
At the high walls of the city
And the well-closed city-gate.
"In his den the fox is hiding,

He has barred his hole most firmly,
But the peasants will unearth him,"
Fridli said, of Bergalingen.
" Forward ! I will be your leader !"
Drums were beating the assault now,
Heavy muskets cracking loudly ;
Through the powder-smoke ran shouting
All these hordes against the town-gate.
On the walls to best advantage
Had the Baron placed his forces ;
And was tranquilly then looking
At the crowd of wild assaulters.
" 'Tis to be regretted," thought he,
" That such strength is idly wasted.
Out of these strong country lubbers
One might form a splendid regiment."
His command is heard : " Now fire !"
The assaulters then were welcomed
With a well-aimed thundering volley,
And they fled in all directions ;
Like a swarm of crows dispersing,
When the hail-shot flies among them.

And not few of them had fallen.
'Neath an apple-tree was lying
By the shore one who spoke feebly
To a comrade passing by him :
" Greet from me my poor old mother,
Also my Verena Frommherz.

ELEVENTH PART.

Say, she can with a good conscience
Marry the tall Uickerhans now.
For, poor Seppli here is staining
The white sand with his true heart's blood!"

Whilst this happened by the town-gate,
Some were trying if the city
Could be entered by a back-way.
On the Rhine below were lying
Fishing-boats beside a cabin,
Where in traps they caught the salmon.
There another crowd streamed onward.
An audacious lad from Karsau
Led them; for, he knew each byway
Near the river, and had often
Many fish at night-time stolen
From the nets of other people.
In three fishing-boats, well manned, thence
Were they rowing up the river.
Willow-trees and heavy brushwood,
And a bend there in the river
Saved them from discovery.
Where the garden of the castle
On arched walls is far projecting
O'er the Rhine, they stopped their barges,
And quite easy was the landing.

On the roof of the pavilion
Which once Fludribus had painted

Sat the black cat Hiddigeigei.
With surprise the worthy cat saw
Spear-heads far below him glistening;
Saw a man, too, upward climbing
On the stone wall, tightly holding
With his teeth a shining sabre;
And how others followed after.
Growling said then Hiddigeigei:
" Best for a wise cat it would be
Ever to remain quite neutral
To man's foolish acts of daring;
But I hate these boorish peasants,
Hate the smell of cows and stables.
If they triumph, woe to Europe;
For, it would destroy completely
The fine atmosphere of culture.
Now look out below, you fellows!
Since the geese by cries of warning
Saved the Capitol of Rome once,
Animals are taking interest
In the history of the world."

Up he sprang in furious anger,
Curved his back, his hair all bristling,
And commenced a caterwauling
Fit to take away one's hearing.

On the jutting turret standing,
Faithful Anton heard this wauling,

And involuntarily looking
Toward that way: "Good heaven!" said he,
"In the garden is the enemy."
Quick his signal-shot brought other
Men-at-arms, along with Werner,
Who placed quickly his few fighters:
"Stand thou here—thou there—don't hurry
With your fire!" His heart beat wildly:
"Ha, my sword, maintain thy valour!"
Shallow was the castle's moat then,
Well-nigh dry, and 'mid the rushes
Glisten many swords and spear-heads.
Daring men are climbing upward
O'er the tower's crumbling stone-work.
Muskets cracking, arrows flying,
Axe-strokes 'gainst the gate are ringing,
Everywhere attack, and shouting:
"Castle thou wilt soon be taken!"
And between, the fall of bodies
In the moat is heard—much blood flows.
By the gate cries out young Werner:
"Well done, Anton! Now take aim at
That dark fellow on thy left hand;
I'll attend unto the other.
Steady now! They are retreating!"

Thus the first attack proved fruitless,
And with bloody heads drew back now
The assaulters, seeking shelter,

'Midst the chestnut-trees' dense thicket.
Scornful words now reach the castle :
"Coward knights, faint-hearted servants,
Keep behind the walls, protected.
Just come out to honest combat
If you've courage." "Death and Devil !"
Werner shouted. "Let the bridge down !
Spears at rest ! Now onward !—Mock us ?
In the Rhine with these damned scoundrels !"

Down the bridge fell rattling loudly ;
Far ahead went Werner rushing,
Right into the crowd ; ran over
Just the fellow who did guide them.
"When the sword gets dull, thou rascal,
With my fist alone I'll kill thee."
In the crowd he sees a sturdy
Soldier, with a weather-beaten
Face, bold and defiant-looking.
He had served with Wallenstein once,
And now fought for these mean peasants
From mere love of strife and bloodshed.
"Taste my steel now, gray old warrior,"
Cried young Werner, as his sword swung
Whizzing through the air to strike him.
But the soldier's halberd parried
Werner's stroke : "Not badly done, lad !
Here my answer !" Blood was dripping
From young Werner's locks ; his forehead

Showed a deep wound from the halberd.
But the one who swung it, never
Gave a second stroke ; his own throat,
Where by armour not protected,
Being cut by Werner's weapon.
Three steps backward then he staggered
Sinking : " Devil, stir thy fire !
Hast me now !" Dead lay the soldier.

Werner, thy young life guard well now !
Raging were the peasants, thronging
In great crowds around this handful.
'Gainst a chestnut-tree now leaning
Weak, but still his life defending,
Stood young Werner ; round him rallied,
Brave and faithful, all the servants.
Save him, God ! The wound is bleeding,
From his hand the sword falls slowly,
Dimmed his eyes are, and the enemy
At his gory breast is aiming.
Then—all may go well yet—
From the castle rings distinctly,
As if for a charge, the trumpet ;
Then a shot—one falls ; a volley
Follows. " Onward !" so the Baron
Now commands, and wildly flying
Tear the peasants to the Rhine.
Cheer up, Werner, friends are coming,
And with them comes Margaretta !

When the fight below was raging,
To the terrace she ascended,
And she blew—herself not knowing
Why she did it—in the anguish
Of her soul, the battle signal
Used in the Imperial army,
Which she'd learned in happy moments
In the honeysuckle-arbour.
It was heard by those returning
With the Baron from the town-gate;
And the maiden's war-cry made them
Hurry quickly to the rescue
Of those fighting in the garden.
Woman's heart, so gentle, timid,
What gave thee such courage then?

"God, he lives!" she bent now softly
Over him who 'neath the chestnuts
There on the green sward was lying,
Stroked the fair locks, lank and bloody,
From his brow: "Hast fought right bravely!"
Half unconscious gazed young Werner;
Did he then behold a vision?
Closed his eyes, and on two muskets
To the castle he was borne.

TWELFTH PART.

YOUNG WERNER AND MARGARETTA.

In the castle's chapel dimly
Was a flickering lamp-light burning,
Shining on the altar-picture,
Whence the Queen of Heaven looked down
With a gracious pitying smile.
'Neath the picture hung fresh gathered
Roses and geranium-garlands.
Kneeling there prayed Margaretta:
"Sorely tried one, full of mercy!
Thou who givest us protection,
Care for him who badly wounded
Lies now on a bed of anguish;
And bestow on me forgiveness
If thou thinkst it very sinful
That he fills my thoughts alone."

Hope and trust their light were shedding
In her heart as thus she prayed.
And more cheerful Margaretta

Now ascended up the staircase.
On the threshold of the sick-room
Was the gray old doctor standing,
And he beckoned her to come there.
Judging what most likely would be
The first question she would ask him,
He then said with voice half muffled:
" Fear no more, my gracious lady;
Fresh young blood and youthful vigour
From such wounds not long can suffer,
And already gentle slumber,
Messenger of health, doth soothe him.
He to-day can take an airing."
Spoke and left; for, his attention
Many wounded men were craving,
And he hated useless gossip.

   Softly entered Margaretta
Now the sick-room of young Werner,
Bashful and yet curious whether
All was true the doctor told her.
Gently slumbering lay young Werner,
Pale in youthful beauty, looking
Like a statue. As if dreaming,
He lay holding, o'er his forehead
And his healing wound, his right hand,
As one who from glaring sunlight
Wishes to protect his eyes;
Round his lips a smile was playing.

TWELFTH PART.

Long on him gazed Margaretta—
Long and longer. Thus in old times
In the forest of Mount Ida
Gazed the goddess, fair Diana,
On Endymion the sleeper.
Pity held her eye a captive ;
Ah, and pity is a fruitful
Soil for love's sweet plant to grow in.
From a tiny seed 'tis spreading
In this ground so rich and fertile,
Which it permeates completely
With its thousand fibrous rootlets.

Thrice already Margaretta
To the door her way had wended,
But as many times returning
She at last approached the bedside.
On the table stood a cooling
Potion, medicines in bottles ;
But she neither touched the cooling
Potion nor the other bottles.
Timidly she bent there o'er him,
Timidly and hardly breathing,
Lest her breath might wake the sleeper.
Long she gazed at his closed eyelids
And involuntarily stooping,
With her lips——But who interprets
All the strange mysterious actions
Of a first sweet loving passion?

Well-nigh can my song conjecture
That she really wished to kiss him;
But she did not; startled sighing,
Turned abruptly—like a timid
Fawn she hurried from the chamber.

Like a man who, long accustomed
To the gloom and damp of dungeons,
Seems bewildered when beholding,
For the first time free fair Nature:
"Hast thou not, O sun, grown brighter?
Has the sky not deeper colours?"
And his eyes are nearly dazzled
By the light so long denied him:
Thus returns the convalescent
Once again to life and vigour.
Fresher, warmer, rosier visions
Rise before his raptured glances,
Which he greets with fond rejoicing.
"World, how fair thou art!" was also
Dropping from the lips of Werner,
As on the broad steps he slowly
Now descended to the garden.
Leaning on his staff, he stood long
Quiet, basking in the sunbeams
Playing o'er the fragrant flowers,
Drew a long breath, and then slowly
Stepped upon the garden-terrace.
On the stone-seat in the sunshine

He sat down now. Bees were humming,
Butterflies were lightly flying
'Mid the verdant chestnut-branches,
Out and in, like tavern-goers.
Green, pellucid, gently rushing,
Bore the Rhine its waters onward;
And a pine-raft filled with people,
Snake-like, swiftly sped toward Basel.
Near the shore, up to his knees stood
In the river there a fisher,
Singing gently to himself thus:

"Peasant comes with spears and muskets,
Peasant storms the forest-city,
Peasant will now fight with Austria:
Peasant! you will find that will
Make much heavier the bill;
Take your purse and pay the joke!
Seven florins seemed too much then,
One-and-twenty must thou pay now.
Soldiers quartered are dear guests too;
Then the plaisters from the surgeons:
Peasant! you will find that will
Make much heavier the bill;
Take your purse and pay the joke!"

Gaily gazed young Werner o'er the
Lovely landscape and the river;
But he stopped his contemplations.

On the wall with sunlight flooded
He beheld a shadow gliding,
As of curls and flowing garments—
Well did Werner know this shadow.
Through the shrubbery came smiling
Margaretta; she was watching
Hiddigeigei's graceful gambols,
Who then in the garden-arbour
With a wee white mouse was playing.
With his velvet paws he held it
Tight, and like a gracious sovereign
Looked down on his trembling captive.

From his seat rose up young Werner
Bowing lowly and with reverence.
Over Margaretta's cheeks spread
Ever-changing rosy blushes.
"Master Werner, may God bless you,
And how are you? You were silent
Such a long time, so with pleasure
Shall I hear your voice once more."

"Since my forehead made acquaintance
Lately with the enemy's halberd,
Hardly knew I," answered Werner,
"Where my life and thoughts had flown to.
O'er me lay thick clouds of darkness;
But to-day in dreams an angel
To my side descended, saying:

Thou art well, arise, be happy
That thou hast thy health recovered.
And it was so. With a firm step
Thus far have I come already."
Now again fair Margaretta's
Cheeks were like the blush of morning.
When the dream young Werner mentioned,
Bashfully she turned her head ; then
Playfully she interrupted :
"I suppose you are now looking
At the battle-field ; indeed it
Proved a hot day, and I fancy
Still I hear the roar of battle.
Do you still recall, you stood there
By yon tree, and there a dead man
Lay beneath those blooming elders?
Where the gossamer so lightly
Through the air in threads is flying,
Spears and halberds then were glittering.
There, where still you see the traces
Of fresh plaster on the stone-wall,
Broke those peasants through when flying.
And, my good sir, over yonder
Then my father loudly scolded,
That a certain person headlong
Had into such danger plunged."

"Death and——but forgive, my lady,
That well-nigh I swore," said Werner.

"They were mocking us; and others,
If they please, may keep their temper.
When I hear such stinging speeches,
Then my heart burns, my fist clenches:
Fight! no other means I know of;
Fight I must, e'en should the whole world
Go to atoms with a crash.
Through my veins there flows no fish-blood;
And to-day, though somewhat feeble,
In the same case, I should stand there
By the chestnut-tree again."

"Wicked man," said Margaretta,
"That a fresh stroke from a halberd
Should be crossing your old scar, and
That——but do you know who suffered
Keenly for your daring conduct?
Do you know whose tears were flowing?
Would you once more give the order:
Lower drawbridge! if I begged you:
Werner stay and do remember
The poor suffering Margaretta?
If I——," but she was not able
Further to spin out her sentence.
What the mouth spoke not, the eyes said;
What the eyes said not, the heart did.
Dreamily young Werner lifted
Unto her his raptured gaze:
"Am I dying, or is doubly

My young life to me now given?"
In each other's arms they flew then,
Sought each other's lips with ardour,
And transported, pressed upon them
Love's first kiss, so sweet and blissful.
Golden-purple streamed the sunlight
Through the shady trees' high summits,
Down upon two happy beings—
On young Werner's pallid features,
On the lovely blushing maiden.

Love's first kiss so sweet and blissful!
Thinking of thee, joy and sorrow
Both steal o'er me; joy, that also
I have once thy nectar tasted,
Sorrow, that but once we taste it!
For thy sake I wished to cull from
Language, all the fairest flowers,
For a wreath unto thine honour;
But, instead of words rose visions
Clear before me, and they led me
Far to float o'er time and space.
First I soared to Eden's garden,
When the new-born world was lying
In its pristine youthful freshness,
When its age by days was reckoned.
Evening came, a rosy light spread
O'er the sky, while in the river's
Waves the sun to rest sank slowly;

On the shore, in merry frolic,
Graceful animals were playing.
Through the shady paths 'neath palm-trees
The first human couple walked.
Wide through space they gazed in silence,
'Mid the holy peace of evening;
In each other's eyes they looked then,
And their lips did meet.
Then I saw before me rising,
Visions of quite different aspect;
Dark the sky, rain-storm and lightning,
Mountains bursting, from the dark depths
Foaming waters rushing upward.
Flooded over is the ancient
Mother Earth, and she is dying.
To the cliffs the waves are rolling,
To the old man and his consort,
To the two last living mortals.
Now a flash—I saw them smiling,
Then embracing, without speaking,
Ever kissing. Night then—roaring,
Did the flood engulf these beings.
This I saw, and well I know now,
That a kiss outweighs all language,
Is, though mute, love's song of songs.
And when words fail, then the singer
Should be silent; therefore silent
He returns now to the garden.
 On the stone steps of the terrace

Lay the worthy Hiddigeigei;
And with great amazement saw he,
How his mistress and young Werner
Were each other fondly kissing.
Grumbling said he to himself then:
"Often have I meditated
On great problems hard to settle,
Which my cat-heart fully fathomed;
But there's one which yet remaineth
Quite unsolved, uncomprehended:
Why do people kiss each other?
Not from hatred, not from hunger,
Else they'd bite and eat each other;
Neither can it be an aimless
Nonsense, for they are in general
Wise, and know well what they're doing.
Why then is it, I ask vainly,
Why do people kiss each other?
Why do mostly so the youthful?
And why mostly so in Spring-time?
Over all these knotty questions,
I intend to ponder further,
On the gable-roof to-morrow."

Margaretta plucked some roses,
Took then Werner's hat, and gaily
With the fairest ones adorned it.
"Poor pale man, till there are blooming
On your own cheeks just such roses,

On your hat you'll have to wear them.
But now tell me, wherefore is it
That I do so dearly love you?
Not a word you ere have spoken,
That could show me that you loved me.
Sometimes only shy and bashful
Did you raise at me your glances,
And sometimes you played before me.
Is it, then, your country's custom,
That a woman's love is won there,
Without words by trumpet-blowing?"

"Margaretta, sweetest darling,"
Said young Werner, "could I venture?
You appeared to me so saint-like,
In your flowing, snow-white garments,
At the feast of Fridolinus.
'Twas your glance which made me enter
In your noble father's service;
And your favour was the sunshine
Which my daily life illumined.
Ah! there by the mountain-lake once,
On my head was placed a garland.
'Twas love's crown of thorns you gave me,
And in silence I have worn it.
Could I speak, O could the homeless
Trumpeter his yearnings utter
Boldly to fair Margaretta?
Unto you as to an angel,

Who is guarding us poor mortals
Did I look in silent worship,
And I wished in your dear service
Here to die beneath the chestnuts.
From that fate you have preserved me,
Unto life and health restored me,
Made my life now doubly precious,
As I know your love adorns it.
Take me then ! Since you did give me
That first burning kiss, I only
Live through you, belong to you now,
Margaretta—ever thine !"

" Thine, yes, thine," said Margaretta ;
" What stiff barriers are erected
By our words ! Belong to you now—
What a solemn cold expression.
Ever thine ! 'tis thus love speaketh.
No more you ; *thou*, heart to heart pressed,
Lips to lips, that is his language ;
Therefore, Werner, let another
Kiss now seal it"—and their lips met.
In the sky the moon first shineth,
Then by countless stars is followed ;
So the first kiss, when once given,
Is by hosts of others followed.
But how many were by stealth robbed
And paid duly back with interest,
All this doth my song keep secret.

Poetry and dry statistics
Are, alas, not on good terms.
Also Anton came now hurrying
Through the garden with a message:
"The three ladies from the convent,
Who the first of May went with us
To the fishing, send their greeting
To your gracious ladyship, and
Also make most kind inquiries
For the health of Master Werner,
Who, they trust, will soon amend."

THIRTEENTH PART.

WERNER SUES FOR MARGARETTA.

NIGHT, how long and full of terror!
When thou bring'st not to the weary
With thy shades refreshing slumber,
And sweet dreams to comfort him.
Restlessly his thoughts are delving
In the past's great heaps of rubbish,
Where they rake up many fragments
Of his former life, and nowhere
Can his eyes abide with pleasure;
Only gloomy spectres rise up,
Which the sunlight soon would banish.
Unrefreshed, next to the future
Roves the mind from which sweet sleep flies;
Forges plans, takes resolutions,
Builds up proud and airy castles;
But like owls and bats are flying
All around them hosts of doubts which
Drive away all hope and courage.

From the tower-clock struck midnight.
On his couch was lying sleepless
Werner in the turret-chamber;
Through the window beaming faintly
Fell a narrow ray of moonlight,
While beneath the Rhine did rush.
And the sleepless brain of Werner
Is by dream-like visions haunted.
Once it seemed to him like Sunday;
Bells are pealing, horses neighing,
Toward the Schwarzwald goes a wedding,
He walks at the head as bridegroom,
By his side is Margaretta;
And she wears a wreath of myrtle.
In the village loud rejoicings,
And the roads and village street are
All with flowers overstrewn.
In his priestly robes is standing
By the church-door the old Pastor
Blessing, beck'ning him to enter——
But the vision's thread broke off here
For a new one: He imagined
At the door there was a knocking;
And now enters the odd figure
Of his dear old friend Perkéo,
With his red nose shining brightly
In the dimly-lighted chamber;
And he speaks with husky voice thus:
"Oh, my lad, with love don't meddle!

Love's a fire which consumeth
Him who kindles it, completely ;
And thou art no charcoal-burner !
Come then home to the clear Neckar,
Come with me to my old wine-tun,
Which contains good stuff sufficient
All thy love-flames to put out."

   Next he seems to be transported
To an Eastern field of battle.
Cries of Allah, sabres whirring ;
And he soon strikes down a Pashaw
From his horse, and brings the crescent
To the general, Prince Eugene,
Who then claps him on the shoulder :
" Well done, my Imperial captain ! "
From the battle-field his dreaming
Flies back to the days of childhood,
And his nurse sings in the garden :
   "Squirrel climbs up on the blackthorn,
Squirrel goes up to the tree-top,
Squirrel falls into his grave.
Had he not so high ascended,
Then his fall had been less heavy,
Had not broken then his leg."

   Thus disturbed by all this dreaming,
Werner sprang up of a sudden,
With long strides walked through his chamber ;

And his mind was troubled always
By the same portentous question:
"Shall I ask the Baron for her?"
Love well-nigh appeared to him now
Just like stolen fruit; he felt that,
Like a thief, before the day broke,
He had better leave the castle.
But just then the sun was rising,
With the beauty of a bridegroom
In the blush of early morning.
"Be ashamed, my heart, great coward!
Yes, I'll ask him," cried young Werner.

At his breakfast sat the Baron
Poring deeply o'er a letter
Which the day before was brought him
By a messenger from Suabia,
From the Danube; where through narrow
Valleys the young stream is flowing,
And steep limestone rocks are rising
From the water which reflects them
With their verdant crowns of beech-trees;
Thence the man had come on horseback.
And the letter read as follows:

"Does my comrade still remember
His old Hans von Wildenstein?
Down the Rhine and Danube many
Drops of water have been flowing,

Since we in that war together
Lay before the bivouac-fire;
And I see it by my son's growth,
Who is now a strapping fellow—
Four-and-twenty years he reckons.
First a page unto his highness
The Grand Duke of Würtemberg;
Then to Tübingen I sent him.
If I by his debts can judge well,
Which I had to pay for him there,
He must have vast stores of knowledge.
Now he stays with me at home, at
Wildenstein; is hunting stags here,
Hunting foxes, hares and rabbits;
But sometimes the rascal even
Hunts the peasants' pretty daughters.
So 'tis time to think of taming
Him beneath the yoke of marriage.
If I err not, you, my friend, have
Just a daughter suited for him.
With old comrades 'tis the custom
Not to beat around the bush, but
Go straight forward to the business.
So I ask you, shall my Damian
Start upon a tour of courtship
To your castle on the Rhine?
Answer soon. Receive the greetings
Of thy Hans von Wildenstein!
 " Postscript: Do you still remember

That great brawl we had at Augsburg,
And the rage of wealthy Fugger,
The ill-humour of his ladies,
Two-and-thirty years ago?"

    With great effort tried the Baron
His friend's writing to decipher,
Spent a good half-hour upon it
Ere he came to its conclusion.
Smiling said he then: "A Suabian
Is a devil of a fellow.
One and all they are unpolished,
And coarse-grained is their whole nature;
But within their square-built noddles
Lie rich stores of clever cunning.
Many stupid brainless fellows
Might from them obtain supplies.
Truly my old Hans now even
In old age is calculating
Like the best diplomatist.
For, his much encumbered, rotten
Owl's-nest out there on the Danube,
Would be well propped up and rescued
By a good rich marriage-portion.
Still his plan is worth considering;
For, the name of Wildenstein is
Well known all throughout the Empire,
Since they followed as crusaders

In the train of Barbarossa.
Let the younker try his chance then!"

   Werner with most solemn aspect,
Dressed in black, the room now entered;
Sadness lay on his pale features.
In good humour spoke the Baron:
" I was wishing just to see you,
For I want you to be ready
With your pen, and as my faithful
Secretary write a letter,
And a letter of importance.
There's a knight who lives in Suabia
Questioning me about my daughter;
Asks her hand from me in marriage
For his son, the younker Damian.
Write him then, how Margaretta
Daily grows in grace and beauty;
How she——but I need not tell you.
Think you are an artist—sketch then
With your pen a life-like, faithful
Portrait, not a jot forgetting.
Also write, to his proposal
I do offer no objection,
And the younker, if he pleases,
May come here and try his fortune."

   " May come here and try his fortune,"
Said young Werner, as if dreaming,

Mumbling to himself—when grimly
Said the Baron: "What's the matter?
You have now as long a visage
As a protestant old preacher
On Good Friday. Is the fever
Coming once again to plague you?"
Gravely answered him young Werner:
"I, my lord, can't write that letter,
You must find another penman;
For, I come myself as suitor,
Come to ask you for your daughter."

"Come—to ask you—for your daughter!"
In his turn now said the Baron
To himself—he made a wry mouth
As one playing on the jew's-harp,
And he felt a sudden twitching
In his foot from his old enemy
Podagra, and gravely said:
"My young friend, your brain is truly
Still affected with the fever.
Hurry quickly to the garden;
There stands in the shade a fountain,
There is flowing clear cool water;
If you dip your head thrice in it
Then your fever soon will cool."

"Noble lord," now answered Werner,
"Spare your jokes, for you may better

Use them, when the noble younker
Comes here from the land of Suabia.
Calm and free from any fever
Have I on this step decided,
And to Margaretta's father
I repeat the same petition."

Darkly frowning said the Baron :
" Do you want to hear from me then
What your own good sense should tell you ?
Most unwillingly I hurt you
With harsh words; I've not forgotten
That the wound upon your forehead,
Hardly healed yet, you received here
By your ardour in my service.
He who ventures as a suitor
For my daughter first must show me
That he comes of noble lineage.
Nature has set up strict barriers
Round us all with prescient wisdom,
To us all our sphere assigning,
Wherein we the best may prosper.
In the Holy Roman Empire
Is each rank defined most clearly—
Nobles, commoners, and peasants.
If they keep within their circle,
From themselves their race renewing,
They'll remain then strong and healthy.
Each is then just like a column,

Which supports the whole; but never
Should these classes mix together.
Do you know the consequences?
Our descendants would have something
Of each class, and yet be nothing—
Shallow, good-for-nothing mongrels,
Tossed about, because uprooted
From the soil of old tradition.
Firm, exclusive must a man be;
And his course of life already
Must be inborn, an inheritance
Coming down through generations.
Hence our custom does require
Equal rank when people marry;
And I hold as law this custom;
I shall not allow a stranger
To o'erleap this solid barrier,
And no trumpeter shall therefore
Ever woo a noble lady."

Thus the Baron. With great labour
Had he put the words together
Of this solemn and unusual
Theoretical discourse.
Meanwhile Hiddigeigei lying
There, behind the stove, was listening.
At the end assent he nodded,
But in thoughtful meditation
Raised his paw up to his forehead,

Reasoning to himself as follows:
" Why do people kiss each other?
Never shall I solve this question!
I did think at last I'd solved it,
Thought that kisses might be useful
As a means to stop one's talking,
And prevent one from declaiming
Bitter stinging words of truth.'
But, alas, now this solution
Seems, I must confess, erroneous;
Else young Werner long before this
Would have kissed my good old master."

To the Baron said young Werner,
And his voice was growing hollow:
" Much I thank you for this lesson.
'Midst the fir-trees of the mountains,
By the green waves of the river,
In the sunlight of the May-time,
Has my eye been overlooking
All these barriers of custom.
Thanks, that you have thus recalled them.
Also, thanks for all your kindness,
Shown to me while on the Rhine.
Now my time is up, the meaning
Of your words I thus interpret:
'Right about face!' I go gladly.
As a suitor fully equal
I shall here return, or never.

Be not angry then—farewell!"
Spoke, and from the room departed,
And he knew what must be done now.
At the door with troubled glances
Still a long while gazed the Baron :
" I am really sad," he muttered,
" Wherefore is this brave youth's name not
Damian von Wildenstein ? "

Parting, parting, dismal moment !
Who first ever did invent it ?
Surely 'twas a wicked man, far
In the Polar Sea, and freezing
Round his nose the polar wind blew ;
And his shaggy, jealous consort,
Plagued him, so he no more relished
The sweet comfort of the train-oil.
O'er his head he drew a yellow,
Furry sealskin, and then waving
With his fur-protected right hand,
To his Ylaleyka spoke he
First this harsh and mournful sentence :
" Fare-thee-well, from thee I'm parting !"

Parting, parting, dismal moment !
In his turret-chamber Werner,
Was now tying bag and baggage,
Fastening up his travelling knapsack :

Greets the walls of his snug chamber
For the last time, for they seemed then
Just like good old friends and comrades.

Only these he took farewell of;
Margaretta's eyes he could not
For the world then have encountered.
To the court-yard he descended,
Quickly his good horse he saddled.
Hoofs then clatter; a sad rider
Rode forth from the castle's precincts.

In the low ground by the river
Stood a walnut-tree; once more there
Now he halted with his horse,
And once more took up his trumpet;
From his overburdened soul then
His farewell rang to the castle—
Rang out; don't you know the swan's song,
When with death's foreboding o'er him
Out into the lake he's swimming?
Through the rushes, through the snow-white
Water-lilies, rings his death-song:
"Lovely world, I now must leave thee;
Lovely world I die reluctant!"

Thus he blew there. Were those tears which
Glistened brightly on his trumpet,

Or some rain-drops which had fallen?
Onward now; the sharp spurs quickly
In the horse's flanks he presses,
And is flying at full gallop
Round the forest's farthest edge.

FOURTEENTH PART.

THE BOOK OF SONGS.

WERNER went to distant countries,
  Margaretta's heart was blighted;
Some few years will now pass over
  Ere the two are reunited.

But, meanwhile, abrupt transitions
  Are not to my taste, I own;
So with songs, like wreaths of flowers,
  Shall this gap be overstrewn.

YOUNG WERNER'S SONGS.

I.

THE moment when I saw thee first,
　　Struck dumb, I stood there dreaming,
My thoughts ran into harmonies,
　　Which through my heart were streaming.

So here I stand, poor trumpeter,
　　And on the sward am blowing;
In words I cannot tell my love,
　　In music it is flowing.

II.

The moment when I saw thee first,
  The sixth of March, like lightning,
Came quickly from the azure sky
  A flash, my heart igniting.

It burn'd up all that dwelt therein,
  A dire destruction bringing,
But from the ruins, ivy-like,
  My loved one's name was springing.

III.

Turn not thy timid glance away,
   To hide what there doth glisten;
Come to the terrace, while I play,
   And to my music listen.

In vain your efforts to escape,
   I still continue blowing;
With magic speed my tunes take shape
   Into a ladder growing.

On these sweet tones' melodious rounds
   Love gently is ascending;
Through bolt and lock still pierce the sounds
   Which I to thee am sending.

Turn not thy timid glance away,
   To hide what there doth glisten;
Come to the terrace while I play,
   And to my music listen.

IV.

A MERRY piece I blew on the shore,
   How clear my trumpet was pealing!
Above the storm the tones did soar
   Up to the castle stealing.

The water-nymph on her crystal couch
   Hears music through the wild roaring;
She rises up to listen well
   To a human heart's outpouring.

And when she dives to her home below,
   With laughter the fishes she's telling,
"O River-children, one doth see
   Strange things where mortals are dwelling.

There stands someone on shore, in the storm:
   What do you think he's doing?
Blows evermore the same old tune—
   The tune of Love's soft wooing."

V.

Thou Muse of Music, take my thanks,
    Be praise to thee forever,
For teaching me thy Art divine,
    That Art which faileth never.

Though language is a noble thing,
    There are limits to what it expresses;
No speech has uttered yet what lives
    In the soul's most hidden recesses.

It matters not that there are times,
    When words to us are wanting;
For then, within, mysterious sounds
    Our spell-bound hearts are haunting.

It murmurs, hums, it swells and rings,
    Our hearts seem well-nigh breaking,
Till music's glorious hosts burst forth,
    To forms of life awaking.

Oft I should stand before my love
    A stupid bashful fellow,
Were not my trumpet there at hand,
    And love-songs sweet and mellow.

Thou Muse of Music, take my thanks,
Be praise to thee forever,
For teaching me thy Art divine,
That Art which faileth never.

VI.

The skylark and the raven
   Are of a different tribe;
I feel as if in heaven!
   That I am not a scribe.

The world is not so prosy,
   The woods with mirth o'erflow,
To me life seems all rosy,
   My trumpet rings hallo.

And merry tunes 'tis sending
   Forth in a constant flow;
Who finds these sounds offending
   May to the cloister go.

When ink it shall be raining,
   Sand fall instead of snow,
Then, from my sin abstaining,
   I nevermore will blow.

VII.

Where 'neath the bridge the waters foam,
   Dame Trout was swimming downward,
And met her cousin Salmon there:
   "How are you, river-comrade?"

"I'm well," quoth he, "but thought just now:
   If only lightning flashing,
Down there, would strike that stripling dead,
   Him and his trumpet smashing!

The live-long day my fine young sir
   On shore is promenading;
Rhine up, Rhine down, and never stops
   His hateful serenading."

Dame Trout, then smiling, answered him;
   "Dear cousin, you are spiteful,
I, on the contrary, do find
   The Trumpeter delightful.

If you, like him, could but enjoy
   Fair Margaretta's favour,
To learn the trumpet even now,
   You would not deem much labour."

VIII.

I PRAY that no fair rose for me,
  By thy dear hands, be broken;
A slip of holly evergreen,
  Be of our love the token.

The chaplet green with glossy sheen
  O'er the fruit good watch is keeping:
And all will prick who try to pick
  What's for another's reaping.

The gaudy rose, when Autumn comes,
  Finds that her beauty waneth;
The holly leaf her modest green
  Through cold and snow retaineth.

IX.

Her fragrant balm the sweet May night
   O'er hill and vale is breathing,
When through the shrubs with footsteps light
   To the castle I am stealing.
In the garden waves the linden-tree,
   I climb to its green bower,
And from the leafy canopy
   My song soars to the tower:
      "Young Werner is the happiest youth
         In the German Empire dwelling,
      But who bewitched him thus, forsooth,
      In words he won't be telling.
      Hurrah! is all that he will say,
      How lovely is the month of May,
         Dear love, I send thee greeting!"

With joyous trills the nightingale
   On the topmost bough is singing,
While far o'er mountain and o'er vale
   The thrilling notes are ringing.
The birds are looking all about,
   Awaking from their slumber;
From branch, and bush, and hedge burst out
   Glad voices without number:
      "Young Werner is the happiest youth
         In the German Empire dwelling,
      But who bewitched him thus, forsooth,

In words he won't be telling.
Hurrah ! is all that he will say,
How lovely is the month of May,
　　Dear love, I send thee greeting !"

The sounds are heard, are borne along
　By the river downward flowing ;
And from afar echoes the song,
　Fainter and fainter growing.
And through the air of rosy morn
　I see two angels winging,
Like a harp's sweet tones, from Heaven borne,
　I hear their voices singing :
　　" Young Werner is the happiest youth
　　　In the German Empire dwelling,
　　But who bewitched him thus, forsooth,
　　　In words he won't be telling.
　　Hurrah ! is all that he will say,
　　How lovely is the month of May,
　　　Dear love, I send thee greeting !"

X.

Who's clattering from the tower
    To me a greeting queer?
'Tis, in his nest so cosy,
    My friend the stork I hear.

He's preparing for a journey,
    O'er sea and land will hie;
The Autumn is coming quickly,
    So now he says good-bye.

Art right, that thou dost travel
    Where warmer skies do smile;
From me greet fair Italia,
    And also Father Nile.

There in the south are waiting
    Far better meals for thee,
Than German frogs and paddocks,
    Poor chafers and ennui!

Old fellow, God preserve thee,
    My blessing take along;
For thou, at peaceful night-time,
    Hast often heard my song.

And if perchance thou wert not
  Asleep within thy nest,
Thou must have seen how often
  With kisses I was blest.

But be not, pray, a tell-tale,
  Be still, old comrade mine,
What business have the Moors there
  With lovers on the Rhine?

XI.

A SETTLED life I did despise,
    And so to wandering took;
When soon I found, to my surprise,
    A comfortable nook.

But as I lay in rest's soft lap,
    And hoped for long repose,
There broke o'er me a thunder-clap,
    My stay came to a close.

Each year a different plant I see
    Spring up, with beauty clad;
A fool's mad dance this world would be,
    If 'twere not quite so sad.

XII.

To life belongs a most unpleasant feature:
    That not a rose without sharp thorns doth grow,
Much as love's yearning stirs our human nature,
    Through pangs of parting we at last must go.
From thy dear eyes, when I my fate was trying,
    A gleam of love and joy streamed forth to me:
Preserve thee God! my joy seemed then undying,
    Preserve thee God! such joy was not to be.

I've suffered much from envy, hatred, sorrow,
    A weather-beaten wanderer sad and worn:
I dreamt of peace and of a happy morrow,
    When I to thee by angel-guides was borne.
To thy dear arms for comfort I was flying,
    In grateful thanks I vowed my life to thee:
Preserve thee God! my joy seemed then undying,
    Preserve thee God! such joy was not to be.

The clouds fly fast, the wind the leaves is sweeping,
    A heavy shower falls o'er woods and meads:
The weather with my parting is in keeping,
    Gray as the sky my path before me leads.
Whate'er may come, joy's smile or bitter sighing,
    Thou lovely maid! I'll think of naught but thee!
Preserve thee God! my joy seemed once undying,
    Preserve thee God! such joy was not for me.

SONGS OF THE CAT HIDDIGEIGEI.

I.

Honest folks are turning lately
   Their attention to the Muses,
And with ease compose their own songs
   For their daily household uses.

Therefore I shall also try it,
   On light pinions freely winging;
For, who dares deny our talent,
   Takes from cats the right of singing?

If I always run to book-stores
   I shall find it too expensive;
And their gaudy books contain oft
   Naught but trash, weak and offensive.

II.

When through vales and on the mountains
    Roars the storm at midnight drear,
Clambering over ridge and chimney
    Hiddigeigei doth appear.

Like a spirit he stands up there,
    Never looked he half so fair;
Fire from his eyes is streaming,
    Fire from his bristling hair.

And he howls in fierce wild measure,
    An old war-cry caterwauling,
Which is borne off by the storm-wind,
    Like the distant thunder rolling.

Not a soul then ever sees him,
    Each is sleeping in his house;
But far down, deep in the cellar,
    Listens the poor trembling mouse.

For his voice she recognises,
    And she knows that, when in rage,
Most ferocious is the aspect
    Of this valiant feline sage.

III.

From the tower's highest summit
   Gaze I at the world below;
From my lofty seat I'm able
   To observe life's ceaseless flow.

And the cat's green eyes are staring,
   And he laughs within his sleeve,
That those pygmies there are trying
   Such great follies to achieve.

What's the use? Up to my level
   Never can I raise mankind.
Let them follow their devices,
   Small their loss is, to my mind.

For perverted are men's actions,
   And their work is woe and crash.
Conscious of his own great value,
   Grins the cat down on this trash!

IV.

O THE world does us injustice,
    And for thanks I look quite vainly;
For the finest chords of feline
    Nature, it mistakes so plainly.

Thus, if some one falls down drunken,
    And a throbbing like a hammer
Racks his heavy head on waking,
    Germans call it *Katzenjammer.*

Katzenjammer, oh great insult!
    Gentle is our caterwauling;
Only men I hear too often
    Through the streets at night-time bawling.

Yes! they do us great injustice,
    Never can be comprehending
All the deep and morbid sorrow
    Which a poor cat's heart is rending.

V.

HIDDIGEIGEI often has raved with delight,
    The true, good, and beautiful seeking;
Hiddigeigei often felt grief's deadly blight,
    And with tender sad yearnings was weeping.

Hiddigeigei once has felt his heart glow,
    When the fairest of cats he was wooing;
And just as a troubadour's love-songs flow,
    Rang nightly his spirited mewing.

Hiddigeigei many a valiant fight,
    Like the Paladin Roland, was waging;
But men have often belaboured his hide,
    And with dropping hot pitch made him raging.

Hiddigeigei to his sorrow found out,
    That his fair one was false and deceiving
That from a poor insignificant lout
    She was secretly visits receiving.

Hiddigeigei then did open his eyes,
    Left off his pining and yearning;
The world henceforth he learned to despise,
    To his inner self earnestly turning.

VI.

Lovely month of May, how hateful
　To a cat you are, and dreary
Ne'er I thought such din of music
　Could a cat's heart make so weary.

From the branches, from the bushes
　Birds their warbling notes are ringing;
Far and wide, as if for money,
　Men I hear forever singing.

There the cook sings in the kitchen—
　Is love also her head turning?
In falsetto she now screameth,
　That with rage my soul is burning.

Farther upward will I clamber,
　To the terrace slowly wending.
Woe to me, for from the garden
　Are my neighbour's songs ascending.

Even next the roof I cannot
　Find the rest for which I'm pining:
Near me dwells a crazy poet,
　His own verses ever whining.

When despairing to the cellar
  Down I rush the noise escaping;
Ah, above me they are dancing,
  To the pipes, and fiddles' scraping.

Harmless tribe! Your lyric madness
  You'll continue, while there yonder,
In the East, the clouds are gathering,
  Soon to burst in tragic thunder.

VII.

May has come now. To the thinker,
Who the causes of phenomena
Searches, 'tis a natural sequence :
In the centre of creation
Are two aged white cats standing,
Who the world turn on its axis ;
And their labour there produces
The recurring change of seasons.

But why is it in the May month
That my eyes are ever ogling,
That my heart is so impassioned ?
And why is it that I daily
Must be leering sixteen hours
From the terrace, as if nailed there,
At the fair cat Apollonia,
At the black-haired Jewess Rachel ?

VIII.

A STRONG bulwark 'gainst enticements
   I have built on good foundations;
But to the most virtuous even
   Sometimes come unsought temptations.

And more ardent than in youth's time,
   The old dream comes o'er me stealing;
I on memory's pinions soar up,
   Filled with burning amorous feeling.

Oh fair Naples, land of beauty,
   With thy nectar-cup thou cheerest!
To Sorrento I'd be flying,
   To a roof to me the dearest.

Old Vesuvius and the white sails
   On the bay are greeting bringing,
And the olive-woods are gladdened
   By the spring-birds' joyous singing.

To the Loggia slinks Carmela,
   Strokes my beard with soft caresses;
Of all cats by far the fairest,
   Lovingly my paw she presses.

And she looks on me with longing,
　But now hark! there is a howling;
Is the surf thus loudly roaring?
　Or is old Vesuvius growling?

'Tis not old Vesuvius growling,
　For he holds now his vacation.
In the yard, destruction vowing,
　Barks the worst dog in creation—

Barks the worst dog in creation—
　Barks Francesco, loudly yelling;
And my lovely dream's enchantment
　He thus rudely is dispelling.

IX.

Hiddigeigei strictly shunneth
  What his conscience might be hurting;
But he oft connives benignly
  At his fellow-cats' gay flirting.

Hiddigeigei with great ardour
  Makes the mice-hunt his chief duty;
And he frets not if another
  With sweet music worships beauty.

Quoth the wise cat Hiddigeigei:
  Ere it rots, the fruit be plucking;
So, if years should come of famine,
  Memory's paws remain for sucking.

X.

Even a God-fearing conduct,
　　Cannot keep us from declining;
With despair I see already
　　In my fur some gray hairs shining.

Yes, unpitying Time destroyeth
　　All for which we've boldly striven;
For against the sharp-toothed tyrant
　　Nature has no weapons given.

Unadmired and forgotten
　　We fall victims to this power.
Wish I could, with fury raging,
　　Eat both clock-hands of the tower.

XI.

Long past is the time, ere man in his might
    O'er the earth his dominion was spreading;
When the mammoth roamed in his ancient right
    Through the forests which crashed 'neath his treading.

In vain may'st thou search now far and near
    For the Lion, the desert's great ruler;
But we must remember, that we live here
    In a climate decidedly cooler.

In life and in fiction is given no praise
    To the great and the highly gifted;
And ever weaker is growing the race
    Till genius to nothing is sifted.

When cats disappear the mice raise their voice,
    Till they like the others skedaddle;
At last in mad frolic we hear *them* rejoice—
    The infusoria rabble.

XII.

HIDDIGEIGEI sees with sorrow
  To a close his days are drawing;
Death may come at any moment,
  So deep grief his heart is gnawing.

O how gladly I the riches
  Of my wisdom would be preaching,
That in joy as well as sorrow
  Cats might profit from my teaching.

Ah! the road of life is rugged;
  On it rough sharp stones are lying.
Stumbling o'er this path so dreary,
  Sprained and bruised we limp on crying.

Life oft useless wounds is giving,
  For 'tis full of brawls and knavery;
Vainly many cats have fallen
  Victims to an empty bravery.

But for what this constant fretting?
  The young cats are laughing ever,
No advice from me accepting—
  Only suffering makes them clever.

Let us see what they'll accomplish;
  History's teachings are derided:
His sage maxims ne'er to publish,
  Hiddigeigei has decided.

XIII.

Growing weaker, breathing harder,
    Soon I'll feel Death's shadow o'er me;
Make my grave there in the store-house,
    In my former field of glory.

Valiantly all round me slaying
    Fought I like a raging lion;
In his armour clad then bury
    Of his race the last brave scion.

Yes the last, because the offspring
    Will their parents equal never!
They are good but wooden people,
    Not so witty nor as clever.

Wooden are they, thinking solely
    Of the moment, hollow hearted;
Only few still hold as sacred
    The bequests of the departed.

But sometime, when years have passed by,
    In my grave I've long been sleeping,
Then will come the angry cat's howl
    Nightly down upon you sweeping.

Hiddigeigei's solemn warning
    Will you from your slumber waken:
Ever fear the coils of dulness!
    Save yourselves, ye God-forsaken!

SONGS OF THE SILENT MAN.

FROM THE CAVE OF THE GNOMES.

I.

Quiet heart! O ponder lonely,
    Valiant, by no fears assailed;
Only in calm meditation
    Lofty secrets are unveiled.

While the storms of life are raging,
    While mean souls for trifles fight,
Thou on wings of song art soaring
    O'er the mob in purer light.

Leave the dusty road to others,
    And thy soul unsullied keep,
A clear mirror, like the ocean,
    Where the sun has sunk to sleep.

O'er the world's loud bustle rising,
    Soars the eagle lone on high;
Cranes and storks, they flock together,
    But close to the earth do fly.

Quiet heart! O ponder lonely,
    Valiant, by no fears assailed;
Only in calm meditation
    Lofty secrets are unveiled.

II.

LEAVE all commonplace forever,
    Digging deeply, upward soaring;
For rich Nibelungen-treasures
    Lie all ready for exploring.

From the mountains we see shining
    Distant seas and shores of beauty;
While beneath we hear the booming
    Of the gnomes hard at their duty.

Manna-like is spread around us
    Spiritual food abundant;
And before our vision rises
    The old truth with light redundant:

As coarse threads and fine together
    In *one* net are intertwisting,
So the same laws are forever
    For the small and great existing.

But a point comes,—sad confession!—
    Where to pause, our thoughts restraining:
At the limit of perception
    Is mysterious silence reigning.

III.

Past me wander beings pallid,
    Fill the air with words of anguish:
All our doings are invalid,
    Sick and old, we slowly languish.

Have you ne'er the wondrous story
    Found in ancient books related,
Of the spring, wherein the hoary
    Plunged, then rose rejuvenated?

And this fountain is no fiction,
    Within reach of all 'tis flowing;
But you've lost the true direction,
    Farther from its traces going.

In the forests' verdant bowers,
    Where deep calm the soul entrances,
Where on graceful ferns and flowers
    Elves sweep through their nightly dances:

There by stones and moss well hidden,
    Rush the waters from the mountain;
From Earth's bosom springs unbidden,
    Ever fresh, this magic fountain.

There with peace the soul is ravished;
    There the mind regains its powers;
And the wealth of Spring is lavished
    O'er old wounds in blossom-showers.

IV.

Wilt thou know the world more clearly,
    See then what before thee lies;
How from matter and from forces
    The whole fabric doth arise.

Of the fixed forms of creation
    Thou the moving cause must see;
In the changes of phenomena
    Find what lasts eternally.

In presumptuous opinions
    Fresh pure seeds ne'er germinate;
By deep meditation only
    Human minds explore, create.

V.

With the eagle's piercing sight endowed,
  And the heart with hope o'erflowing,
I found myself with a mounted crowd
  To thought's fierce battle going.

The banners high, the lance in rest,
  The enemy's ranks were broken.
On their broad backs, O what a jest,
  To mark a nice blue token!

We came at last to the end of our course,
  O'er our failure in knowledge repining;
Then slowly I turned my gallant horse,
  Myself to silence resigning;

Too proud to believe—my thoughts all free,—
  To the cave as a refuge flying.
The world is far too shallow for me,
  The core is deeper lying.

I for my weapons no longer care,
  In the corner there they lie rusting.
No priggish fool to provoke me shall dare,
  To my valour alone I am trusting.

These owls and bats a look alone
  Suffices to abolish;
Still serveth well an ass's bone,
  The Philistines to demolish.

VI.

Be proud, and thy lot nobly bear,
   From tears and sighs desisting;
Like thee will many others fare,
   While thinkers are existing.

There are many problems left unsolved
   By former speculations;
But when thou art to dust resolved,
   Come other generations.

The wrinkles on thy lofty brow
   Let them go on increasing,
They are the scars which show us how
   Thought's struggle was unceasing.

And if no laurel-crown to thee
   To deck thy brow be given;
Still be thou proud; thy soul so free
   For thought alone has striven.

SOME OF MARGARETTA'S SONGS.

I.

How proud he is and stately !
   How noble is his air !
A trumpeter he's only,
   Yet I for him do care.

And owned he castles seven,
   He could not look more fair.
O would to him were given
   Another name to bear !

Ah, were he but a noble,
   A knight of the Golden Fleece !
Love, thou art full of trouble,
   Love, thou art full of peace.

II.

Two days now have passed already,
   Since I gave him that first kiss;
Ever since that fatal hour
   All with me has gone amiss.

My dear little room, so pretty,
   Where so nice a life I led,
Is now in such dire confusion,
   That it almost turns my head.

My sweet roses and carnations,
   Withered now, for care ye pine!
Oh, I think, instead of water,
   I have deluged you with wine.

My dear lovely snow-white pigeon
   Has no water and no bread;
And the goldfinch in his cage there
   Looks as if he were half dead.

I am putting blue and red yarn
   In my white net as I knit;
And I work in my embroidery
   White wool where it doth not fit.

Where are Parcival and Theuerdank?
　　If I only, only knew!
I believe that I those poets
　　In the kitchen-pantry threw.

And the kitchen plates are standing
　　On the book-case—what a shame!
Ah, for all these many blunders
　　I my love, my love must blame!

III.

Away he is gone in the wide wide world;
    No word of farewell has he spoken.
Thou fresh young player in wood and mead,
Thou sun whose light is my daily need,
    When wilt thou send me a token?

I hardly had time in his eyes to gaze,
    When the dream already had vanished;
Oh Love, why dost thou two lovers unite,
With thy burning torch their hearts ignite,
    When their bliss so soon must be banished?

And where does he go? The world is so large,
    So full of deep snares for a rover.
He even may go to Italia, where
The women, I hear, are so false and so fair!
    May Heaven protect my dear lover.

FIVE YEARS LATER.

WERNER'S SONGS FROM ITALY.

I.

Too well were all things going,
  Therefore it could not last;
My cheeks my grief are showing,
  Misfortune came too fast.

The violet and clover,
  The flowers all are gone.
'Mid frost and snow, a rover
  I wander sad alone.

Good luck will never favour
  The man who nothing dares;
But he who does not waver
  The smile of fortune shares.

II.

A LONELY rock juts upward
   Just by the craggy strand;
The angry foaming waters
   Have torn it from the land.

Now in green waves half sunken
   Defiantly it lies;
The snow-white gulls are flying
   Around it with shrill cries.

There on the heaving billows
   Is dancing a light boat;
The sounds of plaintive singing
   Up to the lone rock float:

"O that I to my country,
   And to my love were borne;
O home in dear old Rhine-land,
   For thee my heart is torn!"

III.

Bewitched I am by the summer night,
  In silent thought I am riding;
Bright glow-worms through the thicket fly
Like happy dreams, which in times gone by
  My longing heart were delighting.

Bewitched I am by the summer night,
  In silent thought I am riding;
The golden stars shine so far and bright,
In the water's fair bosom is mirrored their light,
  As, in Time's deep sea, love abiding.

Bewitched I am by the summer night,
  In silent thought I am riding;
The nightingale sings from the myrtle tree,
He warbles so meltingly, tenderly,
  As if Fate his heart had been blighting.

Bewitched I am by the summer night,
  In silent thought I am riding;
The sea rises high, the waves do frown;
Wherefore these useless tears which down
  The rider's wan cheeks are gliding?

IV.

'Neath the waves the sun is going,
With bright hues the sky is glowing,
Twilight o'er the earth is stealing,
Far-off evening bells are pealing:
    Thee I think of, Margaretta.

On the rocky crag I'm lying,
Stranger in a strange land sighing;
Round my feet the waves are dancing,
Through my soul float dreams entrancing:
    Thee I think of, Margaretta.

V.

Oh Roman girl, why lookest thou
    At me with burning glances?
Thine eye, though beautiful it be,
    The stranger ne'er entrances.

Beyond the Alps there is a grave,
    The Rhine watch o'er it keepeth;
And three wild roses bloom thereon;
    Therein my love-dream sleepeth.

Oh Roman girl, why lookest thou
    At me with burning glances?
Thine eye, though beautiful it be,
    The stranger ne'er entrances.

VI.

OUTSIDE the gates when walking,
   I see of life no trace ;
There is the wide-spread graveyard
   Of the ancient Roman race.

They rest from love and hatred,
   From pleasure, strife, and guilt ;
There in the Appian Way are
   Their tombs of marble built.

A tower greets me, gilded
   By the setting sun's last rays—
Cæcilia Metella,
   At thy proud tomb I gaze.

My eyes are turning northward,
   As 'mid this pile I stand ;
My thoughts are swiftly flying
   Far from this southern land,

On to another tower,
   With stones of smaller size ;
By the shady vine-clad window
   I see my love's sweet eyes.

VII.

THE world lies now encircled
   By the frosty winter night.
No use that by the hearth-stone
   I think of love's sad flight.

The logs will soon be burnt out,
   To ashes all will fall;
The embers will cease glowing,
   That is the end of all.

It is the same old story,
   I think of nothing more
But silence and forgetting—
   Forget what I adore?

VIII.

The crowd it frolics, shouts and sings,
　　Disturbs Rome's usual quiet;
Mad folly high her banner swings,
　　And thronging masks run riot.

Now up and down the Corso pace
　　Gay coaches 'mid wild showers;
The Carnival's great sport takes place,
　　The fight with chalk and flowers.

Confetti and fair roses fly,
　　Bouquets are thickly raining.
That hit—good luck! how glows her eye!
　　Thou art the victory gaining.

And thou, my heart, mirth also show,
　　Forget what thou hast suffered;
Let bygone times and bygone woe
　　With flowers sweet be covered.

IX.

By the clear green Lake of Nemi
  An old maple-tree doth grow;
Through its lofty leafy summit
  The breezes sadly blow.

By the clear green Lake of Nemi
  A young musician lies,
He hums a song, while many
  Tears glisten in his eyes.

On the clear green Lake of Nemi
  The waves so gently flow;
The maple and musician
  Their own minds do not know.

By the clear green Lake of Nemi
  Is the best inn of the land;
Praiseworthy macaroni,
  And wine of famous brand.

The maple and musician
  Are crazy both, I think;
Else they would go there yonder,
  Grow sane by honest drink.

X.

My heart is filled with rancour,
   The storm howls all around;
Thou art the man I want now,
   Thou false Italian hound.

Thy dagger's thrust I parried;
   Now, worthy friend, beware
How from a German sword's stroke
   Thy Italian skull will fare.

The sun's last rays had vanished
   Far from the Vatican;
It rose to shine next morning
   Upon a lifeless man.

XI.

Oh Ponte Molle, thou bridge of renown,
Near thee many draughts have I swallowed down,
   From bottles in wicker-work braided.
Oh Ponte Molle, what is the cause
That I between my glasses now pause,
   Can hardly to drink be persuaded?

Oh Ponte Molle, 'tis strange in truth,
That the lovely days of my vanished youth
   And love's old dream are recurring.
Through the land the hot sirocco blows,
And within my heart the old flame glows,
   Sweet music within me is stirring.

Oh Tiber-stream, oh St. Peter's dome,
Oh thou all-powerful ancient Rome,
   Naught care I for all thou containest.
Where'er in my restless wanderings I rove,
My gentle and lovely Schwarzwald-love,
   The fairest on earth thou remainest!

Oh Ponte Molle, how lovely was she!
And if I thousands of girls should see,
   To love but the one I am willing.
And if ever thy solid pile should bear
The weight of her footsteps, I will swear,
   Even thy cold frame would be thrilling.

But useless the longing and useless the woe,
The sun is too ardent so far to go,
   And flying is not yet invented.
Padrone, another bottle of wine!
This Orvieto so pearly and fine
   Makes even a sad heart contented.

Oh Ponte Molle, thou bridge of renown,
Hast thou on my head called witchcraft down
   For my love-sick and dreamy talking?
A cloud of dust whirls up to the sky,
A herd of oxen now passing by
   Blocks up the way I am walking.

XII.

(Monte testaccio.)

I DO not know what the end will be ;
   O'er the low ground spreads the gloaming,
The ominous bat already I see
   As she starts on her nightly roaming.
On Ponte Molle all is still,
I think the good old hostess will
   Very soon the inn be closing.

A little owl I hear there screech
   In the cypress grove 'tis hiding;
Campagna fogs up there now reach,
   Over gate and city gliding.
They roll and float like ghostly troops
Round Cestius' Pyramid in groups;
   What are the dead there wanting?

Now bursts a light around the hill,
   The leaden gray clouds are fast going;
The full moon's face rises slow and still,
   With envy's yellow hue glowing.
She shines so pale, she shines so cold,
Right into the goblet which I hold;
   That cannot be a good omen.

He who from his sweetheart is torn away,
　Will love her more dearly than ever;
And who doth long in the night-air stay,
　Will catch most surely a fever.
And now the hostess the light puts out,
Felice notte! I back to her shout;
　The bill I'll settle to-morrow.

XIII.

Awaking from my slumber
    I hear the skylark sing;
The rosy morning greets me,
    The fresh young day of Spring.

In the garden waves the palm-tree
    Mysteriously its crown,
And on the distant sea-shore
    The surf rolls up and down;

And azure-blue the heavens,
    The golden sun so bright;
My heart, what more is wanting?
    Chime in with all thy might!

And now pour out thy praises
    To God, who oft gave proof,
He never would forsake thee—
    'Tis thou who kept aloof.

XIV.

To serve, to serve! an evil ring,
   Has this word so harsh and frigid;
My love is gone, my life's sweet Spring;
   My heart, become not rigid.

My trumpet looks so sad to-day,
   With crape around it winding;
In a cage they put the player gay,
   Lay on him fetters binding.

Deep grief and pain infest his way,
   His heart with arrows stinging;
For his daily bread he has to play,
   He can no more be singing.

Who on the Rhine sang to his lyre,
   Of all save joy unheeding,
Is now—sad fate—the Pope's great choir
   In the Sistine Chapel leading.

FIFTEENTH PART.

THE MEETING IN ROME.

Scorching lay the heat of summer
Over Rome, th' Eternal City;
Sluggishly his yellow waters
Rolls the Tiber, rolls them seaward,
Through the sultry air; however,
Not so much from choice, but rather
From a sense of duty, knowing
That it is a river's business.
Deep down at the river's bottom,
Sat old Tiber, and he muttered:

"Oh how slowly time is dragging!
I am weary! Would the end were
Of this dull monotonous motion!
Will no storm ere raise a flood-tide,
To engulf this little country,
And drag all the brooks and rivers,
Also me—the river veteran—

And embrace us all together
In the ocean's mighty bosom?
E'en to wash the walls forever
Of old Rome I find most tedious.
And what matter that this region
And myself are held as classic?
Vanished, turned to dust and ashes,
Are those genial Roman poets,
Who, their brows adorned with laurel,
And their hearts imbued with rhythm,
Formerly have sung my praises.
Then came others, long since vanished,
Others followed in their stead, like
Pictures in a magic lantern.
Well! to me 'tis all the same, if
Only they would not disturb me.
Oh what have these busy mortals
Thrown into my quiet waters,
Quite regardless of my comfort!
Where my nymphs with sacred rushes
Had arranged for me a pillow,
For my usual siesta,
There now lie great heaps of rubbish,
Roman helmets, Gaulish weapons,
Old utensils of Etruria,
And the lovely marble statues
Which once from the tomb of Hadrian
Down upon thick-headed Goths fell;
And the bones all mixed together

Of defenders and aggressors ;
Just as if my river-bed were
An historic lumber chamber.
Oh how sick I am and weary !
Worn-out world, when wilt thou die ?"

Whilst now thus the worthy Tiber
Gave full vent unto his anger
By this discontented grumbling,
There above gay life was surging,
And arrayed in festal garments
Crowds went toward the Vatican.
On St. Angelo's Bridge was hardly
Room enough for all the passers.
Crowding came in Spanish mantles,
Wigs and swords, the grand Signori ;
Then some black Franciscan friars,
Also Capuchins, and common
Roman burghers. Here and there a
Sun-burnt and wild-looking shepherd
Of the near Campagna wore with
Classic grace his tattered garment ;
And among them, with light footsteps,
Walked the lovely Roman maidens,
With black veils, although this covering
Did not hide their fervent glances.
(O how can the glowing sunshine,
Even when its rays are gathered
By adepts in their reflectors,

E'er compare with Roman glances?
Heart which felt their flames, be silent!)

 From the castle of St. Angelo
Flutter gaily many banners,
Bearing all the Pope's insignia,
Both the mitre and the crossed keys,
Giving notice of the feast-day
Kept in honour of St. Peter.

 There before the proud cathedral
Were the sparkling fountains playing;
Through the spray the vivid rainbow
Glitters o'er the granite basins.
And the obelisk gigantic
Of Rameses, King of Egypt,
Looked upon the crowd of people,
In his native tongue lamenting:
 "Most perplexing are these Romans!
In the time of Nero hardly
Did I comprehend their doings;
Now still less I understand them.
But this much I have discovered,
That the climate here is chilly.
Amun-Rè, thou god of sunlight,
Take me home to my old friends there,
To the Sphinx, and let me once more
Hear the prayer of Memnon's column
Through the glowing desert ringing!"

On the broad steps of the Vatican
And beneath the marble columns
Tall Swiss halberdiers are walking
To and fro in keeping watch there.
Clanging through the hall the echo
Of their heavy tread is ringing.
To the gray old corporal turning
Speaks a youthful soldier sadly :
"Fine, indeed, and proud we Swiss are,
And I see no other soldiers
In the streets of Rome as jaunty
As we look with our cuirasses,
In the black, red, yellow doublet.
Many burning glances shyly
From the windows fall upon us;
But the heart is wildly yearning
Homeward, homeward for the mountains,
As at Strasburg on the bulwarks
When the Alpine horn was blowing.
Willingly would I give up all,
Earnest money, silver scudi,
E'en the Holy Father's blessing,
E'en the wine of Orvieto
Which pearls sweetly in the goblet,
Could I once again be chasing
Boldly on their tracks the chamois
O'er the rocks, near avalanches,
On the craggy steep Pilatus;
Or steal gently in the moonlight

Over fragrant Alpine meadows
To the faintly-lighted cottage,
To the dairy-maid, the light-haired
Kunigund of Appenzell;
And then greet the golden sunrise
With a joyful heartfelt jodel.
Oh Saint Peter, thy fine music
I should miss without regretting,
Could I hear again the well-known
Sharp shrill whistle of the marmot
In its lonely Alpine cave!"

On the steps of the cathedral
Stood in crowds close packed together
Elegant and idle dandies,
Holding muster over all the
Carriages and great state coaches
Which came quickly driving up there.
"Do you see the Eminenza
With that round face like the full moon,
With the double chin, he's leaning
On the servant in rich livery?
'Tis the Cardinal Borghese.
He would rather now be sitting
Quiet in the Sabine mountains
In the airy villa by the
Rural beauty Donna Baldi.
He's a man of taste, a scholar;

Loves the classics, and especially
Doth he love the true Bucolic."

"Who is that?" now asked another,
"That imposing-looking person?
Don't you see there what a splendid
Chain of honour he is wearing;
How he shakes his periwig now
Like th' Olympian Jupiter?"
"What, you do not known him?" answered
Then loquaciously another,
" Him, the Chevalier Bernini?
Who has just restored the Pantheon,
Who upon St. Peter's also
Has bestowed such rich adornments,
And the golden tabernacle
Built o'er Peter's grave, which cost more
Than a hundred thousand scudi.
Take your hat off! Since the world was,
Has she seen no greater master,
Nor——" He was then interrupted
By a man with gray moustaches,
Who his shoulder tapped and scornful
Said: "You are mistaken; never
Saw the world a greater bungler!
I say this, Salvator Rosa."

Coaches come, in front postilions;
Splendid uniforms are glittering

And with retinue attended
Steps an aged lady onward
To the portal of the Dome.
 " How she's fading," said then someone,
"The illustrious Queen of Sweden!
Do you still recall her lovely
Looks when first she made her entrance?
Then the Gate del Popolo looked
Just as if built out of flowers;
And as far as Ponte Molle
Came the Romans out to greet her.
Down the long street of the Corso
Unto the Venetian Palace
Were the shouts of joy unending.
Do you see that little hunchback
Standing there, who now is sneezing?
He stands high in grace and favour
As one of the queen's attendants.
He's a scholar of deep learning,
The philologist Naudaeus.
He knows everything that happened,
And sometime ago he even,
Over there at Prince Corsini's,
Danced an ancient Saltarello
To instruct the royal party,
Whose loud laughter was heard plainly
Even far off by the Tiber."

 In the throng now quite unnoticed

FIFTEENTH PART.

Came a heavy lumbering carriage;
In it were two black-robed ladies;
On the box sat worthy Anton
As their coachman, calling loudly:
"Room ye people for the gracious
Lady Abbess and my mistress!"
Called in German, which roused laughter.
With bewildered eyes he looked round
At the foreign scene, and just then
Passing by the queen's attendants,
He beheld a gray old coachman,
And he muttered from his coach-box:
"Don't I know thee, Swedish rascal?
Didst thou not belong once to the
Regiment of Sudermanland?
Do you now expect my thanks here
For the cut you had the kindness
To bestow upon my arm once
In the fight at Nuremberg?
A most marvellous place is truly
This old Rome, for long-forgotten
Friends and foes meet here again!"

On the classic soil of Italy
Now my song greets Margaretta.
Gladly would it strew its fairest
Blossoms on the path to welcome
And to cheer this pallid maiden,
So that smiles might light her features;

For, since Werner left the castle,
Pleasure had become a stranger.
Only once they saw her laughing,
When the Suabian younker came there;
But it was a bitter laughter,
Harsh, discordant as a string sounds
On a mandolin when snapping;
And the younker then returned thence
Single, as from home he started.
Silently the maiden sorrowed
As the months and years sped onward;
Till at last the Princess Abbess,
Filled with pity, told the Baron:
"On our soil your child no longer
Thrives as heretofore, but slowly
Her poor heart from grief is withering.
Change of air oft worketh wonders.
Let me take then Margaretta
With me to the Holy City,
Where in spite of age I'm going;
For, in Chur the wicked bishop
Threatens to deprive our convent
Of our fairest Swiss possessions,
And I shall complain of him there,
Saying to the Holy Father:
"Show me mercy, justly punish
The harsh bishop of the Grisons."
Said the Baron: "Take her with you;
And may Heaven grant its blessing.

That you may bring back my daughter
Rosy-cheeked and happy-hearted."
Thus to Italy they travelled
With old Anton as their coachman.

Now the carriage-door he opened,
And alighting, the old Abbess,
Followed by fair Margaretta,
Walked up to the church and entered.
Margaretta gazed in wonder
At the vastness of the building,
Where man seems reduced to nothing;
At the giant marble columns,
And the dome with gold o'erladen.
In the niche of the great nave stands
The bronze statue of St. Peter,
Which this day in papal vestments
Was arrayed, the gold brocade robe
Hanging stiffly on the statue;
On the head the Bishop's mitre.
And they saw how many people
Kissed the foot of this bronze statue.
Then a papal chamberlain led
Both the German ladies forward
To a seat close by the altar,
Place of honour kept for strangers.
Now was heard the sound of music;
And the Holy Father coming
Through the side-door from the Vatican

Made his entrance to St. Peter's.
Stout Swiss halberdiers were marching
At the head of the procession,
Followed by the celebrated
Singers of the papal choir.
Heavy music-books were carried
By the choristers, some hardly
Strong enough to bear the folios.
Then there came in motley order
Monsignori robed in violet;
Abbots followed then and prelates,
And the canons of St. Peter's,
Heavy looking, their fat figures
Corresponding to their livings.
Leaning on his staff the General
Of the Capuchins walked slowly
For a load of more than ninety
Years was resting on his shoulders;
But his brain was working out still
Many plans with youthful vigour.
With Franciscans from the cloister
Ara cœli also came the
Prior of Pallazuola.
By the shores of Lake Albano,
'Neath the shade of Monte Cavo,
Stands his little monastery,
Peaceful spot for idle dreamers.
On he walked in deep thought buried;
And who knows wherefore his mutterings

Did not sound like prayer, but more like
" Fare-thee-well, Amalia."
After them the choicest portion,
All the cardinals, were walking,
Their long robes of scarlet colour
On the marble pavement trailing.
" Heart, be patient," so was thinking
Cardinal di Ottoboni ;
"Now I'm second to the Pope yet,
But in seven years most likely
I shall mount St. Peter's chair."
Then a train of cavaliers came
With their shining swords, and followed
In strict military order ;
'Twas the Pope's own guard of honour.
And at last the Holy Father
Made his entrance, being carried
On a throne by eight strong bearers.
O'er his head were held by pages
The great fans of peacock-feathers.
Snow-white were his festal garments ;
And his right hand, raised in blessing,
Wore the signet-ring of Peter.
Low the crowd knelt down in silence.

At the foot of the High Altar
The procession had arrived now,
And the Pope held solemn service
Over the Apostle's grave.

Solemnly and gravely sounded
The peculiar choral measures
Which old Master Palestrina
Had in his strict style composed.
And the aged Lady Abbess
Prayed with fervent deep devotion.
But fair Margaretta's glances
Were directed up to heaven,
Whence these solemn strains of music
Seemed to her to be descending.
But her eye was then attracted
To the singers' box—she trembled:
For, amid the group of singers,
Though half hidden by a column,
Stood a stately light-haired figure.
And again she looked now upward;
From her sight the Pope had vanished,
All the Cardinals had vanished,
Likewise all the nine-and-eighty
Burning lamps o'er Peter's grave.
"My old dream, dost thou return then?
My old dream, why dost thou haunt me
Even in these sacred precincts?"

The last notes had died out softly,
And the Holy Mass was ended.
"Oh how pale you look, dear lady!"
Said the aged Lady Abbess.
Take my vial, it will help you,

It contains the finest essence
Which I bought myself in Florence
At the cloister of San Marco."

    The procession of the singers
Passed just then before the ladies.
" God in heaven ! oh have mercy !
Yes, 'tis he ! I know the scar there
On his brow—it is my Werner ! "
Dark before her eyes it grew now,
And her heart was beating wildly.
No more could her feet support her,
And the maiden sank down fainting
On the hard cold floor of marble.

SIXTEENTH PART.

SOLUTION AND END.

INNOCENTIUS the Eleventh
Was kind-hearted; and his dinner
He had just now greatly relished.
At dessert he still was sitting,
And while luscious fruit enjoying,
Said to Cardinal Albani:
" Who was that young pallid lady,
Who this morning in St. Peter's
Fell upon the floor and fainted?"
Answered Cardinal Albani:
" On this subject just at present
I can give no information;
But the Monsignor Venusto
I will ask, for he knows always
What in Rome is daily happening;
Knows what in salons is gossiped,
What the senators are doing,
What is drunk by Flemish artists,

What is sung by Prima Donnas,
Even what the puppet-show is
Playing on the Square Navona.
There is naught the Monsignore
Can't unravel and discover."
E'en before was served the coffee
(At that time this was a novel
Beverage and rarely taken,
Only on the highest feast-days)
Had the Cardinal already
Learnt the facts. He thus related:
  " This pale maiden is a noble
Lady, who has travelled hither
With that German Princess Abbess;
And she saw—most marvellously—
In the church a man this morning,
Whom she once had lost her heart with,
And whom, still more marvellously,
She unto this day is loving,
Notwithstanding and in spite of
Want of noble-birth and titles,
And her father's stern refusal.
And the cause of this her fainting
Is, again most marvellously,
No one else but Signor Werner,
Chapel-master to your Holiness.
This the Monsignor Venusto
Heard to-day, when on a visit

To the Abbess who related
Confidentially these facts."

Then the Pope said: "This is truly
A most strange and touching meeting.
Were the subject not too modern,
And the actors of the drama
Not such semi-barbarous Germans,
Then some poet might win laurels
In the sweet groves of Arcadia,
Should he sing this wondrous meeting.
But I truly take an interest
In the grave young Signor Werner.
Greatly has improved the singing
Of my choir, since he leads it,
And the taste for solemn music;
While my own Italian singers
Care too much for operatic
Tunes of lighter character.
Quietly he does his duty,
Of his own accord ne'er speaking;
Never begs of me a favour;
Never was his hand extended
To receive the gifts of bribery.
Yet examples of corruption
Are more frequent with us, surely,
Than the fleas in sultry summer.
Monsignor Venusto knows this!
Seems to me that this grave German

Is consumed by secret sorrow.
I should really like to know now,
If he's thinking of his love yet?"

Said the Cardinal Albani:
" I well-nigh may answer for this.
In the books kept on the conduct
Of all high and low officials
In the State and Church departments,
It is mentioned as a wonder
That he strictly shuns all women.
First we nourished a suspicion
That his heart had fallen victim
To the charms of the fair hostess
Of the inn near Vale Egeria.
He was seen each evening strolling
Through the Porta Sebastiano,
And outside there is no dwelling
But the tavern just now mentioned.
Thus such nightly promenading
Of one yet in early manhood
Could not but arouse suspicion.
Therefore we once sent two persons
Carefully to track his footsteps,
But they found him 'mid the ruined
Tombs along the Appian Way.
There had once a great patrician
Built a tomb to his freed woman,
Whom he'd brought as a remembrance

From Judæa, at the time of
The destruction of the Temple.
She was called Zatcha Achyba.
There he sat, the spies related;
'Twas a subject for an artist:
The Campagna's sombre landscape;
Moonlight on the marble tombstone;
He his mantle wrapped around him;
Mournfully he blew his trumpet
Through the gloomy lonely silence.
This had brought upon him later
Many mocking jeers like this one:
"Signor Werner is composing
For the Jewess there a requiem."

At this smiled the Holy Father,
And the Cardinals did likewise;
Following these high examples,
All the chamberlains smiled also;
Even Carlo Dolci's features
Now relaxed their gloomy sadness.
And the Pope said: "We must all have
Great respect for this young German.
It were well if many others
Who at night away are stealing,
To the Appian Way were going.
Signor Werner, I assure you,
Stands most high in my good graces,
And to-morrow he shall see it;

For, I recollect, I've granted
Then an audience to the Abbess."

   On the first day of July in
Sixteen hundred seventy-nine, there
Rose the sun with special glory.
Cooling blew the tramontana
Through the cypresses and myrtles
In the Vatican's fair garden;
And the half-parched flowers gladly
Raised their heads, breathed out fresh fragrance.
O'er the bronze gigantic pine-cone,—
Which once Hadrian's museum
Had adorned, and now was living
'Mid the jessamines and roses,
As a pensioner contented,—
Lively lizards swiftly glided,
Snapping at the tiny insects
Ever dancing in the sunshine.
Fountains played, and birds were singing;
E'en the pale old marble statues
With warm life became imbued.
And the satyr, with his reed flute,
Raised his foot as if intending
To go dancing round the garden;
But Apollo's hand waved warning:
"Friend, those times have passed forever;
Thou wouldst only raise a scandal."
Bathed in sunlight, Rome looks smiling

O'er the river at the Vatican;
From the sea of houses, churches,
And fair palaces, the Quirinal
Proudly rises; in the distance
Towers up the Capitolium
In the violet autumn haze.

Through the Boscareccio's verdant
Alleys swept the shining white robe
Of His Holiness, who kindly
To the Abbess and the maiden
Here had granted audience.
And the Abbess gained assurance,
That her lawsuit would be taken
Into prompt consideration.
Then to Margaretta turning,
Said the Pope: " None of the pilgrims
Ever leave Rome without comfort;
So I, as the soul's physician,
Must prevent another fainting."
And he whispered to a servant:
" Go and fetch the chapel-master."

Werner came: to stately manhood
In this southern clime he'd ripened
Since he left, a hopeless suitor,
The old castle in the Rhine-land.

Life's wild whirlpool, since that morning,
Had well tossed him hither thither.
Willingly I would relate here,
How he went to many countries;
How o'er land and sea he travelled;
How he with the Knights of Malta
Cruised against the Turkish corsairs;
Till at last a fate mysterious
Unto Rome had duly brought him.
But my song becomes impatient;
Like a driver who is snapping
At the door his whip, 'tis calling:
"Onward! On to the conclusion!"
Werner came; bewildered gazed he
Twice, yes thrice, at Margaretta,
Gazed at her in utter silence;
But his glances did express more
Than a printed folio volume.
'Twas the glance with which Ulysses
Sitting by the suitors' corpses
Gazed upon his consort, from whom
He by twenty years of wandering
And of suffering had been parted.

Innocentius the Eleventh
Was kind-hearted, a discerner
Of men's hearts. Most kindly said he:

"Those whom Providence united
In His goodness and His wisdom,
Shall no more be separated.
Yesterday when in St. Peter's,
And to-day here in the garden,
I have come to the conviction,
That there is a case here waiting
For my papal interference.

"'Tis indeed a mighty power
Love, a power all subduing;
Than light even more ethereal,
Doth it penetrate all barriers,
And the chair of Peter also
Is not safe from its invasion
When it asks us for our help.

"But it is a pleasant duty
Of the head of Christendom,
To make smooth the path of lovers,
Every obstacle removing,
That true love may be victorious.
And of all the various nations,
'Tis the Germans who beyond all
Keep us busy with such matters.
So the Count of Gleichen brought here
With him a fair Turkish consort
From the Holy Land, though knowing
His own consort still was living.
And our annals make full mention

Of our predecessor's troubles
Brought about by this wild action.
So likewise the most unhappy
Of all knights came here, Tannhäuser:
   " 'Pope Urbano, Pope Urbano,
Heal the sick man held as captive
Seven years within the mountain
Of the wicked goddess Venus!'
But to-day the case is different
And more pleasing; there is nothing
Which conflicts with any canon.
There is only a slight scruple—
If I've heard right—with the Baron.
You, my Werner, have been faithful,———
But I read 'neath all this quiet
Resignation to your duty,
That reluctantly you sang here,
As a caged-up bird is singing.
Oft you've asked for your dismission,
Which I ever did deny you,
And to-day would never grant you,
If it only were the custom,
That the papal chapel-master
Could like other mortals marry.
But in Rome we must keep always,
As you know, traditions sacred;
Palestrina for this reason
Went himself to foreign lands.

"Therefore go with my full favour;
And because the lady's father
Thinks the name of Werner Kirchhof
Much too simple, so I grant you
Knighthood by my sovereign power.
You, I know, care naught about it;
For you by your art ennobled
Think such titles of no moment.
But perhaps the gracious lady
May consider it more proper,
To bestow her hand in marriage
On the Marquis Camposanto
Rather than on Master Werner.
And because I hold the power
Both to bind as well as loosen,
I now solemnly betroth you.
E'en this loveless age rejoices
At examples of devotion.
You have shown one—be then happy,
And receive my papal blessing."

This he spoke with much emotion.
And o'erwhelmed with grateful feelings
Werner knelt with Margaretta
Down before the Holy Father;
And the Abbess wept so freely
That the grass thought it was raining.

SIXTEENTH PART.

With the tears of the good Abbess
Closes now the touching story
Of the young musician Werner
And the lovely Margaretta.

.

But who's wandering late at night-time
Through the Corso, who is stealing
Through that dark and narrow side-street?
'Tis the faithful coachman Anton;
Filled with joy is his whole being.
To give vent unto this feeling
He is going to the wine-house,
To the tavern del Fachino.
And to-night he is not drinking
Country wine in fogliette;
He has ordered a straw-covered
Bottle of good Orvieto
And of Monte Porzio.
Panes are crashing, fragments flying;
For he throws each empty bottle
In his rapture through the window.
Though indignant at the oil-drops
Which upon the wine are floating,
Just like comets in the ether,
Still he drinks and drinks with ardour;
Only while the tavern-keeper
Went to fetch him the sixth bottle

From the cellar, thus he spoke out:
  "Thou, oh heart of an old coachman,
Now rejoice, for soon thou'lt harness
Thy good horses and drive homeward.
From the standpoint of a coachman
Italy is but a mournful
Land, behind in every comfort.
Horrid roads, and frequent toll-gates,
Musty stalls, and oats quite meagre,
Coaches rough! I feel insulted
Every time I see those waggons
Drawn by oxen yoked together.
The first element is wanting
Of a coachman's daily comfort,
'Tis the handy German hostler.
Oh how much I miss those worthies!
Oh how gladly I will welcome
One in pointed cap and apron!
In my joy again to see him
I will hug and even kiss him.
And at home what great surprises
Are in store! Oh never was I
So impressed with the grave duties
Of a coachman as at present.
At a proud trot, such as never
Has been seen in this whole country,
Shall I drive my lord and ladies
Home through Florence and Milan.

"At Schaffhausen, the last station
For our night's rest, I must promptly
Send a messenger on horseback,
And he must alarm the city:
'Put up quickly all your banners,
Load your cannons for saluting,
And erect an arch of honour!'
Then we enter the next evening
Through the ancient gate in triumph,
And my whip I'll crack so loudly
That the town-house windows rattle.
Then I hear the aged Baron
Asking sharply: 'What's the meaning
Of these banners and this uproar?'
From afar I shout already:
'Heaven's blessing rests upon us;
Here a bridal pair are coming,
And, my lord, they are your children.'
This day ne'er shall be forgotten!
In remembrance shall the tom-cat
Hiddigeigei have a genuine
Whole well-smoked Italian sausage.
For the sake of after ages
Must the good schoolmaster make me
A fine poem on this subject;
I don't care, e'en should it cost me
The amount of two whole thalers,
And it must conclude as follows:

" 'From true love and trumpet-blowing
Many useful things are springing ;
For true love and trumpet-blowing
E'en a noble wife are winning.
May true love and trumpet-blowing
Each one find good fortune bringing,
As our trumpeter young Werner,
On the Rhine at old Säkkíngen.' "

THE END.

NOTES.

THE TOWN OF SAKKINGEN, where the scene of this poem is laid, is situated amid beautiful scenery on the outskirts of the Schwarzwald (Black Forest), on the right bank of the Rhine, and on the road from Basel to Constance, about 30 miles above the former place. The town owes its origin to the settlement of St. Fridolinus (as related in the Third Part of the poem), who came here from Ireland in the 6th century, and founded a monastery, afterwards converted into a convent for noble ladies. The settlement was made on an island in the Rhine. In the poem the town is still considered as lying on an island, but according to the legend, St. Fridolinus altered the course of the Rhine, leading its waters entirely to the west side of the island.

The castle of Schoenau, on the site of the old castle of the Baron, the father of the heroine of the story, stands close to the Rhine, and is now the seat of Mr. Theodore Bally, the well-known wealthy and benevolent proprietor of large silk manufactories. He has caused the old tower of the castle to be restored, and intends to adorn its walls with frescoes, representing scenes from the poem.

Page 1.—Michele Pagano, a very popular hotel-keeper in Capri, whose hotel was mostly frequented by German artists. He died only very recently, universally regretted.

Page 3.—The cat Hiddigeigei, the old Baron's cat, with which the reader will become better acquainted as a philosophising cat in the course of the poem.

Page 5.—Amaranth, a poem by Oscar von Redwitz, published a few years before "The Trumpeter of Säkkingen," and at that time very popular, especially with certain classes in Germany.

Page 13.—The Boezberg, a mountain in the Jura, over which the old road from Basel to Zürich led. Now the railroad between the two places pierces it with a tunnel.

——The Hozzenwald, the Hauenstein mountains. See note to page 15.

—— The Gallus Tower, an old tower at the upper extremity of Säkkingen, properly called after St. Gallus, now used as a house of refuge for homeless people.

Page 14.—The graveyard of Säkkingen contains still the tombstone of the hero and heroine of the poem. Their names, as given there, are Franz Werner Kirchhofer and Marie Ursula von Schoenau. The first died in May, 1690, the latter in March of the following year.

Page 15.—The Eggberg is one of the mountains in the Hauenstein country, to the north of Säkkingen. The inhabitants of this country were formerly remarkable for their quaint costumes coming down from the 15th century. The men wore shirts with large frills around the neck, red stomachers, long black jackets, and wide trousers reaching below the knee, and called hozen. Hence the land was called Hozzenland. The dress of the women was also very peculiar, and of many bright colours. These old costumes are now rarely seen.

Page 17.—" The silvery lake," a romantic small lake, half an hour N.W. from Säkkingen. It lies in a hollow on the hills, surrounded by rocks and splendid fir-woods. The lake, which is known by the name of Berg See (mountain lake), is now also called Scheffel See. It is a favourite spot for excursions from far and near, and abounds in fish.

Page 19.—The Feldberg, the highest point of the Schwarzwald.

Page 20.—St. Blasien, formerly a very ancient monastery of Benedictine monks, called thus after St. Blasius, Bishop of Sebaste, whose relics were brought here by one of the early abbots.

Page 21.—"Then appeared as Death and Devil." This is the subject of one of Albrecht Dürer's most celebrated engravings, called Ritter, Tod, and Teufel (the Knight, Death, and the Devil), where the knight rides quietly and unmoved through a gloomy mountain glen, smiling at Death, who holds up an hourglass before him, and taking no notice at all of the droll Devil, who tries to grasp him from behind. The knight is evidently an embodiment of the freer spirit which began to reign then in Germany. The engraving is of the year 1513.

Page 26.—"Far off on the island glisten." The town of Säkkingen with its minster.

Page 30.—Rheinfeld, or rather Rheinfelden, a town on the left bank of the Rhine, about halfway between Säkkingen and Basel, where, during the Thirty Years' War, in the year 1638 several actions took place.

Page 32.—Wehr, a village about six miles from Säkkingen, on the road to Schopfheim, in the neighbourhood of a stalactite cave (Hasler Hoehle) mentioned in the Tenth Part.

Page 38.—Cujacius (Jacques de Cujas), a very distinguished jurist and professor of law in the university of Bourges († 1590). His only daughter, Susanna, became known by her profligate life. But the stories told of her by Catherinot cannot have happened during her father's lifetime, as he died when she was only three years old.

X

Page 43.—Palsgrave Frederic married the Princess Elizabeth, daughter of James the First of England, in 1613. He was afterwards made king of Bohemia by the Protestant princes of Germany, and moved to Prague in 1619. In the year following his army was routed near Prague by the forces of the Catholic League, and he had to fly with his family.

Page 46.—"Of a young and handsome carpenter." The pastor refers here to a popular German song, still often sung by students:

> War einst ein jung, jung Zimmergesell,
> Der hatte zu bauen ein Schloss, etc.

It is the story of a young carpenter who built a castle for a Margrave. During the absence of the latter the Margravine falls in love with the carpenter. The lovers are afterwards surprised by the Margrave, who has a gallows built on which the carpenter is hung.

Page 49.—Clovis (465-511), king of the Franks, was married, while he was still a heathen, to Clotilde, a Christian princess of Burgundy. During the battle at Tolbiac (Zülpich), near Cologne, when sorely pressed by the enemy, the Allemanni, he vowed to become a Christian, if he should gain the victory. After routing and subjugating the Allemanni, the king and many thousands of his people were baptised by the Bishop of Rheims, on the 23rd of December of the same year (496).

Page 50.—"Augusta Rauracorum," Colonia Raurica, afterwards called Augusta Rauracorum, a Roman colony founded in the year 44 B.C., by L. Munatius Plancus. On the site of the Roman town are now two villages, Basel-Augst and Kaiser-Augst, the latter a station on the railroad from Basel to Zürich. Near Basel-Augst the remains of a Roman amphitheatre and of a temple can still be seen.

Page 56.—Count Ursus of Glarus had been converted to Christianity by St. Fridolinus, and, with the consent of his brother Landolph, donated, a short time before his death, all his estates to the new cloister at Säkkingen. When Landolph, after the death of his brother refused to acknowledge his will, Fridolinus was obliged to go to law in order to make good his claim, and after a long litigation was at last notified by the government of Glarus that he would not be able to have his claims settled, unless he could bring the dead Count Ursus himself in court as a witness. Then, the legend says, Fridolinus went, on the day appointed for the court, to Glarus, raised Ursus from his grave, and walked with him to Rankweil (the seat of the court, ten hours from Glarus), where the count gave testimony in regard to his donation. Landolph then not only gave up his brother's estates, but added also a large portion of his own. After that Fridolinus walked back to Glarus with Count Ursus, and committed him again to his grave. The saint, on account of this miracle, is usually portrayed in company with the skeleton of Count Ursus.

Page 58.—Laufenburg, a town six miles above Säkkingen, and situated on the beautiful rapids of the Rhine. A tower of the old strong castle on the Swiss side is still standing.

Page 59.—Beuggen, a town on the Rhine below Säkkingen. The ancient building of the Teutonic order is still standing, and is used now by the Moravians as an institute for children.

Page 71.—The Wiese, a river coming from the Feldberg and flowing into the Rhine a little below Basel. The beautiful valley of the clear rapid river is now much visited, as there is a railroad as far as the town of Zell. This region has become classic through the poet Hebel, who wrote in the Allemannic idiom, still generally spoken in this whole region. At Hausen, the station before Zell, where he was born, a monument has been erected to him. There is also at Schopfheim, the station below Hausen, on a hill called Hebelshoehe, a bust of the poet. The women of this region are remarkable for their large singular-looking caps, to which Scheffel alludes.

Page 76.—This gravel bank, called Field of Fridolinus, is still seen in the Rhine, opposite the castle Schoenau.

Page 80.—Hallau, a village not far from the railroad station Neuhausen, the stopping-place for visiting the falls of the Rhine. The red wine grown there is still very celebrated.

—— The Hohe-Randen, a mountain to the north of Schapfhausen.

Page 85.—Theuerdank, a German poem of the beginning of the 16th century, written by Melchior Pfinzing, the secretary of the Emperor Maximilian, who had planned and sketched the poem himself.

Page 101.—Grenzach, the first German vil'age going from Basel, on the railroad to Säkkingen and Constanz. It is celebrated for the wine grown there.

Page 104.—The Frickthal, in the Swiss canton Aargau, nearly south of Säkkingen.

Page 105.—Schinznach, a village in the canton Aargau, much visited on account of its hot sulphur springs. In the neighbourhood are the ruins of the castle of Hapsburg, the cradle of the imperial house of Austria.

Page 109.—The mountain lake. See note to page 17.

Page 120.—May drink, or May wine, a favourite drink in Germany for the spring-time, made by steeping the leaves of woodroof in the light white wine of the country, and sweetening it with sugar. It is an old custom prevailing already in the 16th century, when the woodroof was added to the wine not only to cheer the heart with its fine aroma, but also for medicinal purposes, as acting on the liver.

Page 135.—Albbruck, a place above Laufenburg on the Rhine, at the mouth of the little river Alb, the valley of which is the most beautiful in the Schwarzwald. Formerly there were here quite important ironworks.

Page 151.—" E'en a common Flemish blacksmith." Quentin Massys (1466–1530), a celebrated Flemish painter, said to have been originally a blacksmith. While such, he fell in love, and in order to gain the maiden's consent as well as her father's (who was an artist) he forsook his trade, devoted himself to painting, and became a great master in his art. On the tombstone which his admirers placed on his grave a hundred years after his death, stands the Latin hexameter :

> Connubialis amor ex mulcibre fecit Apellem !

Page 152.—The Gnome's cave (Die Erdmannshöhle), a stalactite cave near the village of Hasel (whence the cave is called also Haselhöhle), between Wehr and Schopfheim. It can be reached from the former by a walk of half an hour, and is often visited with guides. The first cave, which one reaches through a low passage, is 13 feet high, the next contains a small lake. There is also a little river rushing along under steps, over which one walks. The cave contains, like all caves of this kind, most fantastic stalactite structures, which popular fancy has called the organ, the chancel, the skeleton, &c. Some columns when struck give out tones which sound as thirds. The most interesting part of the cave is called Die Fürstengruft (The Prince's Sepulchre), a large room, 16 feet high, with a stalactite structure resembling a large coffin. Popular superstition has from times immemorial made this cave the haunt of gnomes.

Page 169.—The ancient county of Hauenstein lies between two spurs of the Feldberg, the eastern one coming down to the town of Waldshut on the Rhine, the western one to Säkkingen. It is also called Hozzenland (see note to page 15). The early history of the country is somewhat obscure until the time of the Emperor Rudolph of Hapsburg, when it acknowledged the sovereignty of Austria. In the times of the fight for the German throne between Albrecht of Austria and Adolphe of Nassau, and between Frederick the Beautiful and Ludwig of Bavaria, when Suabia was without a duke and Germany without an emperor, the different villages of the country founded a union (Einung) for their protection. There is still in existence such a union document drawn up in the year 1433. The entire union was divided into eight smaller ones, each of which stood under an elected leader (Einungsmeister). All these eight leaders elected one of their body as speaker (Redmann), who held the leadership of the entire union. By this the Hauenstein peasants were greatly protected in their ancient rights; still the oppression of the Austrian governors (Waldvoegte) often incited revolutions, the most important of which occurred during the Peasants' War in 1525. Others lasted from 1589 to 1614, arising from an impost laid on wine. The poet introduces such a rising here in the course of his story.

Page 206.—The Fuggers are an Augsburg family, who, by their linen-trade and weaving, and afterwards by the purchase of mines in Austria, amassed an enormous fortune, and were raised to the rank of nobles by the Emperor Maximilian. The family attained their greatest splendour under the Emperor Charles the Fifth, who, at the time of the Diet at Augsburg, raised the two brothers then living to the rank of counts.

Page 235.—Katzenjammer, literally translated, cats' misery, the vulgar German expression for the indisposition after a drunken debauch.

Page 255.—Parcival, written by Wolfram von Eschenbach about the year 1200. Theuerdank, a German poem of the 16th century. See note to page 85.

Page 277.—" As at Strasburg on the bulwarks." The Swiss soldier refers here to a popular song :

> Zu Strasburg auf der Schanz,
> Da ging mein Trauern an, etc.

The simple but touching story of a soldier who stands guard on the bulwarks of Strasburg and hears the Alpine horn blown on the other side of the Rhine. Seized with home sickness he swims across the Rhine, but is taken afterwards and shot as a deserter.

Page 278.—The villa of the Cardinal Borghese, Casa Baldi, near Olevano, in the Sabine country, is still in existence, and is now an inn much frequented by artists. It has become celebrated by Scheffel's humorous song, "Abschied von Olevano" (Farewell to Olevano), which he wrote on the spot when leaving there after a long sojourn. It is published in Scheffel's collection of songs, "Gaudeamus."

Page 285.—Cardinal Pietro Ottoboni of Venice, who in 1689 became the successor of Innocent XI. as Alexander VIII.

www.ingramcontent.com/pod-product-compliance
Lightning Source LLC
Chambersburg PA
CBHW030806230426
43667CB00008B/1084